GOD

and the
Problem of Evil

GOD

and the

Problem of Evil

by
Sister Concetta Belleggia, D.S.P., M.A.

ST. PAUL EDITIONS

Nihil Obstat:
    Rev. Richard V. Lawlor, S.J.
    Censor Deputatus

Imprimatur:
    +Humberto Cardinal Medeiros
    Archbishop of Boston

Original title of this dissertation: *Principles for Teaching about God and the Problem of Evil.*
    Grateful acknowledgment is made to the publishers of the following publications for their gracious permission to reproduce quotations from these works:

God and the Permission of Evil, by Jacques Maritain. Translated by Joseph W. Evans, Milwaukee: The Bruce Publishing Co., 1966. Excerpts reprinted with permission of Jacques Maritain Center, University of Notre Dame, Notre Dame, Indiana 46556.

Excerpts from *The Jerusalem Bible,* copyright © 1966 by Darton, Longman & Todd, Ltd. and Doubleday and Company, Inc. Used by permission of the publisher.

The New American Bible, copyright © 1970, by the Confraternity of Christian Doctrine, Washington, D.C. Excerpts used by permission of copyright owner. All rights reserved.

On the Philosophy of History, by Jacques Maritain. Translated by Joseph W. Evans. Clifton, New Jersey: Augustus M. Kelly, Publishers, 1973. Excerpts reprinted with permission of Charles Scribner's Sons, New York, N.Y. 10017.

"Chapter 37" from *On the Truth of the Catholic Faith:* Book One by St. Thomas Aquinas, translated by Anton C. Pegis. Copyright © 1955 by Doubleday & Company, Inc. Reprinted by permission of the publisher.

Excerpts from *On the Truth of the Catholic Faith:* Book Three by St. Thomas Aquinas, translated by Vernon J. Bourke. Copyright © 1956 by Doubleday & Company, Inc. Reprinted by permission of the publisher.

L'Osservatore Romano (English edition), Vatican City (Europe). Excerpts from addresses of His Holiness, Pope John Paul II, reprinted with permission.

Excerpts from the English translation of *The Roman Missal* © 1973, International Committee on English in the Liturgy, Inc. All rights reserved.

Saint Thomas and the Problem of Evil, by Jacques Maritain. Milwaukee: Marquette University Press, 1942. Reprinted with permission of the Marquette University Press, Milwaukee, Wisconsin 53233.

Excerpts from *Summa Theologiae,* by St. Thomas Aquinas. Copyright, 1963, Blackfriars. Used with the permission of McGraw-Hill Book Company.

Cover: V. Mancusi

ISBN   0-8198-3007-0   cloth
        0-8198-3008-9   paper

Copyright © 1980 by the Daughters of St. Paul

Printed in the U.S.A. by the Daughters of St. Paul
50 St. Paul's Ave., Boston, MA 02130

TABLE OF CONTENTS

Introduction

One of the most crucial signs of our times is *atheism*. In fact, just a few hours before this writing, in one of the largest universities in Boston, a visiting professor lectured on *the non*-existence of God.

If it is true, as it is, that the existence of God, the Creator and Lord, can be known with certainty by the natural light of reason from created things, especially by means of causality, how is it that modern philosophers deny it?

The Council Fathers, in the document of the Second Vatican Council, *Gaudium et Spes:* "The Pastoral Constitution on the Church in the Modern World," write:

> Many of our contemporaries have never recognized man's intimate and vital link with God, or have explicitly rejected it. Thus atheism must be accounted among the most serious problems of this age, and is deserving of closer examination.
>
> The word atheism is applied to phenomena which are quite distinct from one another. For while God is expressly denied by some, others believe that man can assert

absolutely nothing about Him. Still others use such a method to scrutinize the question of God as to make it seem devoid of meaning. Many, unduly transgressing the limits of the positive sciences, contend that everything can be explained by this kind of scientific reasoning alone, or by contrast, they altogether disallow that there is any absolute truth. Some laud man so extravagantly that their faith in God lapses into a kind of anemia, though they seem more inclined to affirm man than to deny God. Again some form for themselves such a fallacious idea of God that when they repudiate this figment they are by no means rejecting the God of the Gospel. Some never get to the point of raising questions about God, since they seem to experience no religious stirrings nor do they see why they should trouble themselves about religion.[1]

But, concluding their reflection, the Council Fathers say: "Moreover, atheism results not rarely from a violent protest against the evil in this world."[2]

Jacques Maritain, too, the world-renowned modern Thomist (1882-1973), in his book, *God and the Permission of Evil*, attributes the origin of many forms of contemporary atheism to the problem of evil. He writes:

In proportion as the conscience of men, under the very influence of Christianity, became more sensible of the dignity of the human person and of the outrages which are inflicted on him by evil, while on the other hand the dimensions of evil, of injustice, of cruelty, of all the kinds of crimes at work in history were more and more revealed to it in depth as well as in extension (today one has only to open the newspaper to see the iniquities which pride or stupidity linked to hardness of heart cause to be committed at the four corners of the earth)—in proportion, consequently, as such a process developed, *the problem of evil* has taken on a more tragic importance for the human conscience. *It is this problem which is at the origin of many forms of atheism*, at the origin also of what one could call in many the bewildered Christian conscience.[3]

This dissertation, therefore, *God and the Problem of Evil*, will be an examination and study of the problem of evil in terms of its nature, its causes and its relationship to God, as these have been analyzed and investigated in the writings of Maritain, who, in turn, seeks his own support in the treatment offered by St. Thomas. The catechetical teacher of today very often is confronted with the question of the problem of evil and why God, if He exists, does not do anything about it. Answers are given which might not be convincing, due to a rationalistic way of thinking characteristic of the present era. Thus, in order to give reasons based on Christian philosophy first of all, as well as on theology, a good percentage of this dissertation will be direct quotations from the works of Maritain, the greatest disciple today of St. Thomas Aquinas.

This dissertation will be a philosophical and theological approach to the truth that all that exists outside God is the work of His divine goodness and wisdom; that God created a *good* world; that He keeps all created things in existence; that He, through His providence, protects and guides all that He has created; that He created man *good* and *free* and conferred on man a supernatural destiny and the means to reach it. Above all, it will prove that all that man does *which is good* comes from God, and all that man does *which is evil* comes from man himself.

As can be seen, the focus here is *moral evil*, that is, sin.[4] It will be shown, following the two luminaries, Maritain and St. Thomas, that God is in no degree the *inventor* of the evil that the creature does. In no degree and in no respect does God *initiate* sin. The *initiative* and the *invention* of sin have their origin in the rational creature. Moreover, God *has not the idea of evil*,[5] because the ideas of God are creative, while instead evil is *non-being*, even though it is *real*, and so real that it disfigures the free act of man.

This work will not be complete if the following truths are not added: that God is present everywhere; that His knowledge is infinite; that therefore He knows perfectly the *evil* that man does; and that He will "reward each one according to his behavior."[6] Also, man's personal responsibility is great, but God, in His infinite power and mercy, always makes evil work for good as St. Paul says: "Now we know that for those who love God all things work together unto good."[7]

What is needed today, more than ever before, is catechesis directed to all levels. Pope John Paul II writes:

> Many pre-adolescents and adolescents who have been baptized and been given a systematic catechesis and the sacraments still remain hesitant for a long time about committing their whole lives to Jesus Christ. ....Even adults are not safe from temptations to doubt or to abandon their faith, especially as a result of their unbelieving surroundings. This means that

"catechesis" must often concern itself not only with nourishing and teaching the faith, but also with arousing it unceasingly with the help of grace.[8]

In what follows, the purpose is to pursue this analysis and study of the problem of evil in terms of its nature, its cause, and its relationship to God. But, first, it is necessary to summarize both Maritain and Saint Thomas with regard to the "place" of the human person; that is, his relationship to God, to God's providence, to God's created world and to God's law. This is necessary in order to set the proper stage for the responses offered by Maritain to the questions concerning the "nature" and the "cause" of evil; and, at the same time, reveal the Thomistic support for Maritain's responses.

As a fitting and most needed conclusion, it will be shown that God, besides being most innocent in regard to the problem of evil, is also most merciful, because He sent His only-begotten Son to suffer and die for man's sin. And He forgives repentant sinners, and in His mercy and power always makes evil work out for good. Therefore, a scriptural approach will follow the philosophical one, mindful of the strong words of Pope John Paul II in his Apostolic Exhortation, *Catechesi Tradendae*, in regard to the integrity of the content:

> What kind of catechesis would it be that failed to give their full place to man's creation and sin; to God's plan of redemption and its long, loving preparation and realization; to the incarnation of the Son of God; to Mary, the Immaculate One, the Mother of God, ever Virgin, raised body and soul to the glory of heaven, and to her role in the mystery of salvation; to the mystery of lawlessness at work in our lives and the power of God freeing us from it; to the need for penance and asceticism; to the sacramental and liturgical actions; to the reality of the Eucharistic Presence; to participation in divine life here and hereafter, and so on?[9]

The value of this study for the investigator is her specific mission in the Church. In fact, as a member of the Daughters of St. Paul, the investigator works with the media of social communication to evangelize. Thus, to evangelize effectively, she feels obliged to know the signs of the times, of which the most crucial today is atheism. In particular, the reason for special and personal interest in this subject is the investigator's desire to present, on the one hand, the innocence, goodness and mercy of

God in regard to moral evil, and, on the other hand, the personal responsibility of the rational creature for moral evil and his salvation in Christ Jesus, the Way, the Truth and the Life.

What follows is a review of the most closely related literature:

God and the Permission of Evil, by Jacques Maritain. Translated by Joseph W. Evans. Milwaukee: The Bruce Publishing Co., 1966. A philosophical work, giving a clear explanation for the grave matter of evil. In it the author maintains an essentially Thomist position, but he also views the problem of evil and suffering in human life in the light of new and urgent questions, and in so doing gives a new and valuable philosophical perspective to the problem.

On the Philosophy of History, by Jacques Maritain. Translated by Joseph W. Evans. Clifton, New Jersey: Augustus M. Kelly, Publishers, 1973. An approach to the philosophy of history mainly divided as follows: 1) the philosophy of history in general, i.e., from the point of view of the theory of knowledge; 2) axiomatic formulas or functional laws, i.e., universal statements manifesting the stability in the course of history of certain basic fundamental characteristics; 3) typological formulas or vectorial laws, i.e., statements which deal with the very growth of history and which manifest typical direction in the historical development; 4) God and history, or rather: God and the mystery of the world.

Saint Thomas and the Problem of Evil, by Jacques Maritain. Milwaukee: Marquette University Press, 1942. The Aquinas Lectures given by Professor Jacques Maritain. In these lectures, he maintains the principal characteristics of Thomistic teaching concerning evil and emphasizes two points: first, the meaning of the existence of evil in this world; second, the cause of evil where free will is concerned.

Existence and the Existent, by Jacques Maritain. Translated by Lewis Galantiere and Gerald B. Phelan. Garden City: Image Books, 1956. An essay on the existentialism of St. Thomas Aquinas, the only authentic existentialism, as the author explains, completely different from the "existentialist" philosophies of today.

In addition, the related parts of the *Summa Theologiae* and the *Summa Contra Gentiles* are used for comparison, contrast, and evaluation.

The World
Rational Creatures
and
Their End

In his work, *The Philosophy of History*, Maritain has written:

> What is the world? In a most general sense, it is the ensemble of created things, or of *all that which is not God.* Then, in a more restricted sense, it is our *material* and visible universe. And then it is our *human* and moral universe, the cosmos of man, culture, and history, as they develop on earth, with all the mutual relations and ten-

sions involved. The world, thus, constitutively belongs to the order of nature; and it is from the mere point of view of nature that we shall consider it first. Let me observe, in addition, that this *human* sense of the word *cosmos, mundus, the world*, is most appropriate: for in the material universe man, as an intelligent and free agent ("in the likeness of God") is *par excellence* the existent which is not God.[1]

Having defined the nature of the world in both a general and a more restricted sense, Maritain speaks of a threefold natural end in its history. He states that there is, first of all, a real temporal and terrestrial end in the history of the world, one which is even mentioned in the Bible:

>   ...What can we say concerning the natural end of the world? In my opinion,...a first aspect of the natural end of world history is mastery over nature and the conquest of autonomy for mankind. We read in Genesis, 1:28: "And God blessed them, saying: Increase and multiply, and fill the earth, and subdue it and rule over the fishes of the sea, and the fowls of the air, and all living creatures that move upon the earth." These words point to mastery over nature: *subdue the earth*.[2]

Then he speaks of a perfecting natural end of man:

> A second aspect is the development of the multifarious immanent or spiritual, self-perfecting activities of such a being [man], especially knowledge—all the various degrees of knowledge—and creative activity in art, and, as concerns moral activity, that progress in the knowledge of natural law.[3]

Lastly, Maritain presents a third aspect of the natural end of the world, specifically man himself:

> Finally, a third aspect of this natural end of the world may be brought out—I mean, the manifestation of all the potentialities of human nature. This, too, would follow from the fact that man is not a pure spirit but a spirit united to matter. It is normal for a spirit to manifest itself. And because man has so many hidden potentialities, it is normal that he reveal progressively this inner universe which is man himself.[4]

Maritain concludes that the world continually advances toward its threefold end, but he also points out that there is a progress both in the direction of good and at the same time in the direction of evil.

Turning now from Maritain to his support in St. Thomas, it must be noted that the latter beautifully states how the intellectual and rational beings were made very special among all God's other creatures:

> ...they do stand out above other creatures, both in natural perfection and in the dignity of their end. In the order of natural perfection, only the rational creature holds dominion over his acts, moving himself freely in order to perform his actions.[5]

Also:

> Only the intellectual creature is by nature free.[6]

St. Thomas further explains how God has special care for His rational creatures, while He governs the others as man's instruments:

> First of all, then, the very way in which the intellectual creature was made, according as it is master of its acts, demands providential care whereby this creature may provide for itself, on its own behalf; while the way in which other things were created, things which have no dominion over their acts, shows this fact, that they are cared for, not for their own sake, but as subordinated to others. That which

THE WORLD, RATIONAL CREATURES... 25

is moved only by another being has the formal character of an instrument, but that which acts of itself has the essential character of a principal agent.[7]

Through His Providence, God guides all that He has created, St. Thomas teaches, for the sake of man:

As a thing is acted upon in the course of nature, so is it disposed to action by its natural origin. Now, we see that things do go on in the course of nature in such a way that intellectual substance uses all others for itself; either for the perfecting of its understanding, since it contemplates the truth in them; or for the exercise of its power and the development of its knowledge, in the fashion of an artist who develops his artistic conception in bodily matter; or even for the support of his body which is united with the intellectual soul, as we see in the case of men. Therefore, it is clear that all things are divinely ruled by providence for the sake of intellectual substances.[8]

Moreover, intellectual creatures, due to their intellectual nature, are closer to God's likeness, so even for this reason they are particularly cared for by God:

...Of all the parts of the universe the more noble are intellectual creatures, since they come closer to the divine likeness. Therefore, intellectual creatures are governed by divine providence for their own sakes, while all others are for the intellectual ones.[9]

God gave man the highest end—He created man for Himself:

> ...an intellectual nature alone attains to God in Himself, that is, by knowing and loving Him.[10]

To man alone God gave a rational and immortal soul, and made him capable of personal acts:

> The personal acts of a rational creature are properly the acts that stem from the rational soul. Now, the rational soul is capable of perpetual existence, not only in function of the species, as is the case with other creatures, but also in an individual sense....
>
> This is why, though all things are subject to divine providence, the care of man is especially attributed to it in Sacred Scripture, in the text of the Psalm (8:5): "What is man that Thou art mindful of him?"[11]

God, through His providence, guides man to his divinely given end by directing his personal acts:

God takes care of each nature according to its capacity; indeed, He created singular creatures of such kinds that He knew were suited to achieving the end under His governance. Now, only the rational creature is capable of this direction, whereby his actions are guided, not only specifically, but also individually. For he possesses understanding and reason, and consequently he can grasp in what different ways a thing may be good or bad, depending on its suitability for various individuals, times, and places. Therefore, only the rational creature is directed in his acts by God, individually as well as specifically.[12]

God also gave man the honor of helping other things reach their natural end:

Furthermore, the rational creature is subject to divine providence in such a way that he is not only governed thereby, but is also able to know the rational plan of providence in some way. Hence, it is appropriate for him to exercise providence and government over other things. This is not the case with other creatures, for they participate in providence only to the extent of being subordinated to it. Through this possession of the capacity to exercise providence, one may also direct and govern his own acts. So, the rational creature participates in divine providence, not only by being governed passively, but also by governing actively, for he governs himself in his personal acts, and even others.[13]

A RATIONAL PLAN
FOR THE RATIONAL CREATURE

To help His rational creature reach his divinely given end, it was appropriate for God to give man a law. This law that God gave man is a rational plan and a rule of operation:

> It is apparent...that it was necessary for law to be divinely given to man. Just as the acts of irrational creatures are directed by God through a rational plan which pertains to their species, so are the acts of men directed by God inasmuch as they pertain to the individual, as we have shown. But the acts of irrational creatures, as pertaining to the species, are directed by God through natural inclination, which goes along with the nature of the species. Therefore, over and above this, something must be given to men whereby they may be directed in their own personal acts. And this we call law.

. . . .

...Since law is simply a certain rational plan and rule of operation, it is fitting that law be given only to those beings who know the rational character of their work. Now, this is proper only to a rational creature. Therefore, it was appropriate that law was given to the rational creature only....

. . . .

It is said in Jeremias (31:33): "I will give my law in their bowels"; and in Osee (8:12; Douay modified): "I shall write my manifold laws for them."[14]

The chief purpose of the divinely given law is man's adherence to God in love. Thus, by this law man is ordained to know his Creator with his intellect and to love Him with his will:

Now, it is quite clear that man chiefly clings to God through love. For there are two things in man by which he is enabled to cling to God, namely, intellect and will. For by means of the lower parts of his soul he cannot cling to God, but only to inferior things. Now, the union which is effected through the intellect is completed by the union which pertains to the will, because through his will man in some way rests in that which the intellect apprehends.... Hence it is said in Matthew (22:37-38): "the first and greatest commandment of the law is: Love the Lord thy God."[15]

Another purpose of the divinely given law is to make man good:

> ...Again, the end of every law, and above all of divine law, is to make men good. But a man is deemed good from his possession of a good will, through which he may put into act whatever good there is in him. Now, the will is good because it wills a good object, and especially the greatest good, which is the end [God]. So, the more the will desires such a good, the more does a man advance in goodness....

> Besides, man's goodness stems from virtue, "for virtue is what makes its possessor good." Hence, law also intends to make men virtuous, and the precepts of law are concerned with acts of the virtues.[16]

By living according to the divine law man reaches his divinely given end and also perfect happiness. St. Thomas affirms this when, writing on the felicity of man, he concludes all his proofs thus: "man's ultimate felicity consists only in the contemplation of God."[17]

> Again, as we have said, law is a rational plan of divine providence, in its governing capacity, proposed to the rational creature. But the governance of God, as providence, conducts individual beings

to their own ends. Therefore, man is chiefly ordered to his end by the divinely given law. Now, the end for the human creature is to cling to God, for his felicity consists in this, as we have shown above. So, the divine law primarily directs man to this end: that he may cling to God.

Hence, it is said in Deuteronomy (10:12): "And now, Israel, what doth the Lord thy God require of thee: but that thou fear the Lord thy God, and walk in his ways, and love him, and serve the Lord thy God, with all thy heart and with all thy soul?"[18]

And in the Psalms we read: "How good is God to Israel, to them who are of a right heart!"[19]

Finally, by the divinely given law men are also ordered to love their neighbor, for the following specific, good reasons:

—Because they share in the ultimate end, which is happiness:

> The next point after this [love of God] is that divine law intends the love of neighbor.
>
> For there should be a union in affection among those for whom there is one common end. Now, men share in common the one ultimate end which is happiness, to

which they are divinely ordered. So, men should be united with each other by a mutual love.[20]

—Because they are loved by God:

Again, whoever loves a person must, as a consequence, also love those loved by that person and those related to him. Now, men are loved by God, for He has prearranged for them, as an ultimate end, the enjoyment of Himself. Therefore, it should be that, as a person becomes a lover of God, he also becomes a lover of his neighbor.[21]

—Because they need one another:

Besides, since "man is naturally a social animal," he needs to be helped by other men in order to attain his own end. This is most fittingly accomplished by mutual love which obtains among men. Therefore, by the law of God, which directs men to their ultimate end, mutual love is prescribed for us.[22]

—Because they seek tranquillity and peace and need to be strengthened in their already existing natural love for one another:

Moreover, so that man may devote his time to divine matters, he needs tranquillity and peace. Now, things that are potential disturbances to peace are removed principally by mutual love. So, since the divine law orders men in order that they may devote themselves to divine matters, it is necessary for mutual love to be engendered among men by divine law.

Furthermore, divine law is offered to man as an aid to natural law. Now, it is natural to all men to love each other. The mark of this is the fact that a man, by some natural prompting, comes to the aid of any man in need, even if he does not know him. For instance, he may call him back from the wrong road, help him up from a fall, and other actions like that: "as if every man were naturally the familiar and friend of every man." Therefore, mutual love is prescribed for men by the divine law.

Hence it is said in John (15:12): "This is my commandment: that you love one another": and in 1 John (4:21): "This commandment we have from God, that he who loveth God love also his brother"; and in Matthew (22:39) it is said that the second commandment is: "Love thy neighbor."[23]

At the conclusion of this first chapter, having followed the development of the treatment of Maritain and St. Thomas, one can conclude: that God has the creative ideas of good only; that He created a good world; that He created the rational creature good and free; that He gave man a special divine purpose: to know and love Him and his neighbor, and thus to be virtuous and perfectly happy; that God also gave man a divine law, in order to show him the way and means to his divine end and to perfect happiness.

2

The Nature of Evil
and Its Cause

EVIL IN THE HISTORY OF MAN AND OF THE WORLD

In the history of humanity, as first recorded in the Old Testament, a person is presented with the philosophical and theological truth of a *good* world, created by one God, an all-powerful God, a just and merciful God, a God who remains always with His people. But the reader of the Bible, while fascinated by the doctrine of creation, is even more impressed by the history of salvation unfolding in the midst of the history of the world. He sees the salvific undertakings of God, starting already at the outset, constantly present in the history of man. They shine forth especially in the history of Israel and lead to the supreme event of Christ's death and resurrection. After the Patriarchs and the Prophets, the promised Messiah is shown in His concrete existence, in His admirable human life, and especially as the all-holy Son of God:

> No one has ever seen God;
> it is the only Son, who is nearest to the Father's heart,
> who has made him known.[1]

The Son was sent by the Father into a world full of sin as Savior and Redeemer of all men: "God in Christ was reconciling the world to himself, not holding men's faults against them, and he has entrusted to us the news that they are reconciled."[2]

The Bible affirms that everything that God created was *good:*

> God said: "Let there be light," and there was light....
> God said, "Let there be a vault in the waters to divide the waters in two." And so it was....
> God said, "Let the waters under heaven come together into a single mass, and let

dry land appear." And so it was.... *And God saw that it was good....*

. . . .

God said, "Let us make man in our own image, in the likeness of ourselves...."

God created man in the image of himself,

in the image of God he created him,

male and female he created them....

God saw all he had made, and indeed it was very good.[3]

Immediately after, the Bible also presents evil—sin—as it appeared in the world for the first time:

Yahweh God gave man this admonition, "You may eat indeed of all the trees in the garden. Nevertheless, of the tree of the knowledge of good and evil you are not to eat, for on the day you eat of it you shall most surely die."

. . . .

...The serpent was the most subtle of all the wild beasts that Yahweh God had made. It asked the woman, "Did God really say you were not to eat from any of the trees in the garden?" The woman answered the serpent, "We may eat the fruit of the trees in the garden. But of the fruit of the tree in the middle of the garden God said, 'You must not eat it, nor touch it, under pain of death.'" Then the serpent said to the woman, "No! You will not die! God knows in fact that on the day you eat it your eyes will be opened and you will be like gods, knowing good and evil." The woman saw that the tree was good to eat and pleasing to the eye, and that it was desirable for the knowledge that it could give. So she took some of its fruit and ate it. She gave some also to her husband who was with her, and he ate it.

...The man and his wife heard the sound of Yahweh God walking in the garden in the cool of the day, and they hid from Yahweh God among the trees of the garden. But Yahweh God called to the man, "Have you been eating of the tree I forbade you to eat?" The man replied, "It was the woman you put with me; she gave me the fruit, and I ate it." Then Yahweh God asked the woman, "What is this you have done?" The woman replied, "The serpent tempted me and I ate."

Then Yahweh God said...to the woman:

> "I will multiply your pains in child-bearing,
> you shall give birth to your children in pain.
> Your yearning shall be for your husband,
> yet he will lord it over you."

To the man he said, "Because you listened to the voice of your wife and ate from the tree of which I had forbidden you to eat,

> Accursed be the soil because of you.
> With suffering shall you get your food from it
> every day of your life.
> It shall yield you brambles and thistles,
> and you shall eat wild plants.
> With sweat on your brow
> shall you eat your bread,
> until you return to the soil,
> as you were taken from it.
> For dust you are
> and to dust you shall return."

The man named his wife "Eve" because she was the mother of all those who live. Yahweh God made clothes out of skins for the man and his wife, and they put them on. Then Yahweh God said, "See, the man has become like one of us, with his knowledge of good and evil. He must not be allowed to stretch his hand out next and pick from the tree of life also, and eat some and live for ever." So Yahweh God expelled him from the garden of Eden, to till the soil from which he had been taken. He banished man, and in front of the garden of Eden he posted the cherubs, and the flame of a flashing sword, to guard the way to the tree of life.[4]

Vatican II confirms:

Although he was made by God in a state of holiness, from the very dawn of history man abused his liberty, at the urging of the Evil One. Man set himself against God and sought to find fulfillment apart from God.[5]

Thus, from the very beginning of humanity, the existence of evil in the world became a reality, and, from that time on, evil kept taking on greater dimensions, until the time of the deluge:

Yahweh saw that the wickedness of man was great on earth, and that the thoughts in his heart fashioned nothing but wickedness all day long. Yahweh regretted having made man on the earth, and his heart grieved. "I will rid the earth's face of man, my own creation," Yahweh said, "and of animals also, reptiles too, and the birds of heaven; for I regret having made them." But Noah had found favor with Yahweh.

This is the story of Noah:

Noah was a good man, a man of integrity among his contemporaries, and he walked with God. Noah became the father of three sons, Shem, Ham and Japheth. The earth grew corrupt in God's sight, and filled with violence. God contemplated the earth; it was corrupt, for corrupt were the ways of all flesh on the earth.

God said to Noah: "The end has come for all things of flesh; I have decided this, because the earth is full of violence of man's making, and I will efface them from the earth. Make yourself an ark out of resinous wood....

"For my part I mean to bring a flood, and send the waters over the earth, to destroy all flesh on it, every living creature under heaven; everything on earth shall perish. But I will establish my Covenant with you.... From all living creatures, from all flesh, you must take two of each kind aboard the ark, to save their lives with yours."[6]

Today human conditions remain the same: today's history is a history of sin. But, men of the present time are not like the believers of the past. Secularized civilization too often diverts minds from God and from their spiritual heritage. Modern philosophers, intellectuals and leaders of public opinion have become hostile to religion, and in their works they make God less present, less needed, and, above all, less able to explain the moral evils of all kinds that affect humanity: injustice, hatred, crime, war and all other iniquity. They have even reached the point of accusing God of being responsible for such evils. Why, they ask, is there so much evil in the world if God is so good?... Does God really exist? Enraged as they are at the abominations in the world, they have even denied His existence.

Effective help may be given to individuals, as well as to educators and parents in their duty of instruction, by trying to examine the tragic reality of moral evil—first in its nature, and then in its cause.

EVIL AS A "PRIVATION" AND AS A "DEPRIVATION"

Throughout the history of the Church, evil has been treated as a privation and a deprivation in relationship to the "good." St. Thomas and J. Maritain are no exceptions to this affirmation.

For a more detailed treatment in their writings, it is best to appeal, first, to human experience for aids to greater understanding. A comparison will help: experience shows that in order for one to draw a straight line, one ought to use a ruler. But, experience also shows that one does not have to use the ruler if his decision is against it. In the latter case, the non-use of the ruler results in a crooked line rather than a straight line.

A first principle has thus been identified: there is a determinate relationship between the ruler and the ruled: the straightness of the line *depends on the ruler and its use*. Without the use of the ruler and with a claim to independence from the use of the ruler, only a crooked line (the absence of straightness) can be drawn.

A corollary to this principle follows from its admission and use: the responsibility for the crooked line must be attributed to the one who has refused to use the ruler. Thus, the neglect of the use of the ruler has predetermined the existence of a crooked line or the absence of straightness.

By analogy, therefore, "privation" and "deprivation," in their relationship to *evil* and *good*, will signify the predetermination of the evil act as a privation or deprivation in the good, *by one who has refused to use the ruler of reason and God's rule of operation or divine law in the performance of his human acts*. The privation and/or the deprivation that is the "evil" is injected into the world of activity by him who refuses to admit a dependence on the rule of reason and the rule of God. Thus, the human person is the cause of evil (the crooked line or act).

A _____ The straight line *needs* the ruler.

B _____ The crooked line needs no ruler. Without the ruler, only a crooked line can be drawn.

C Results in the straight line; or the ruled act; or the good act.

Use of ruler

D Results in crooked line; that is, the absence of straightness, or the evil act.[7]

Non-use of ruler

Now returning to the treatments of St. Thomas and Jacques Maritain, one notes Maritain writing thus:

> With regard to the metaphysics of evil, St. Thomas appropriates and develops the great themes made classical by St. Augustine: evil is neither an essence nor a nature nor a form nor an act of being. Evil is an absence of being; it is not a mere negation, but a *privation*: the privation of the good that should be in a thing.[8]

Then, continuing the explanation of the *how* of the real existence of evil, Maritain says:

Evil does exist in things, it is terribly present in them. Evil is real, it actually exists like a wound or mutilation of the being; evil is there in all reality, whenever a thing —which, insofar as it is, and has being, is good,—is deprived of some being or of some good it should have. Thus evil exists *in good*, that is, the bearer of evil is good, insofar as it is being. And evil works *through good*, since evil, being in itself a privation or non-being, has no causality of its own. Evil is therefore efficacious not by itself but through the good it wounds and preys upon as a parasite, efficacious through a good that is wanting or is deflected, and whose action is to that extent vitiated.[9]

Pursuing this theme, Maritain asks:

What is thus the power of evil? It is the very power of the good that evil wounds and preys upon. The more powerful this good is, the more powerful evil will be, —not by virtue of itself, but by virtue of this good. That is why no evil is more powerful than that of the fallen angel. If evil appears so powerful in the world of to-day, that is because the good it preys upon is the very spirit of man,—science itself and moral ideals corrupted by bad will.[10]

Following the teaching of St. Thomas, Maritain compares moral and physical evil, asserting that the former. is far worse than the latter:

> Another point of doctrine in which St. Thomas faithfully takes up again the great tradition of Plato and St. Augustine, is that the evil which is a fault, and which affects man's will and his liberty, making him evil himself and offending the Principle of his being, is a greater evil than the one which consists in suffering, and which merely affects nature in us, without causing us to swerve from the line of our ultimate destiny, which is supratemporal, and without being opposed, as St. Thomas puts it, "to Good increate, to the Good of God Himself, to the fulfillment of the divine will and divine love by which divine good is loved for itself, and not only as it is participated in by the creature." It is better to be punished than to be guilty.[11]

St. Thomas himself had compared good with evil, affirming their constitutive differences only in the field of morals:

> Good and evil are not constitutive differences except in the field of morals, where acts get their specific character from the end, the objective of will, on which morality depends. Since good has the character of end, so is it that good and evil are specific

differences for morality—good of itself, evil as setting aside the due end. Yet this rejection of the proper purpose does not itself constitute a type of moral action except as conjoined to an undue attachment; as indeed in nature we never find a thing deprived of one substantial form except because another is present. So then the evil which is a specific difference in morality is some good involving being deprived of another good: the end for an intemperate man, for example, is not to be devoid of that value which consists in acting intelligently, but to obtain the sensuously pleasurable outside the order of reason. Hence evil is a differential constitutive, not for its own sake, but by reason of the good with which it is bound.[12]

Further on, St. Thomas defines evil thus:

An evil is a privation of a good, and good chiefly and of itself lies in perfection and actuality....
Now since good is the objective of will, evil, which is the privation of good, is found in a special manner in rational creatures possessing will. ...A person is held responsible and to blame for a shortcoming that falls under the control of the will.[13]

In the same question he also writes:

> The perfection of the universe requires immortal substances and mortal. Likewise it requires that some can cease to be good, and in consequence on occasion do. Such defection from good is precisely what evil is.[14]

THE CAUSE OF EVIL

Having considered evil in its *nature*, that is, as a "privation" of a due good and as a "deprivation," a closer look will be given now to evil in its *cause*.

The principle cited above, namely, that which identifies the relationship between the ruler and the ruled and which establishes clearly the fact that the *agent* who is willfully responsible for the drawing of a crooked line rather than a straight one (by his refusal to use the ruler) is the *initiator* or *the cause* of the crookedness in the line. In other words, the personal agent who claims this independence from the necessity to use the ruler to draw the straight line is the responsible agent who first brings into existence the "absence of straightness" that deprives the line of its straightness.

Applied to the problem of evil in order to seek the *cause* of the "privation" which actually deprives the human act of its full goodness which would be added to it from the *proper use of the rule of reason and the rule of God's law*, the cause of the "evil" or "deprivation" of the human act is identified: it lies in the personal agent, the human person, who brings to existence the absence of the proper and good act which deprives the good act of its fullness of being.

The human person is, therefore, the cause of the entry of evil into the world. This conclusion follows the teaching of the Church which affirms the fact that the human person is the first actor in the line of evil, whereas, he can only be a *second actor* in the line of the good act since he requires a subordination to the rule of reason and the rule of the law of God in order to do the good act—an act which has as its first agent the rule of reason and the rule of God's law.

MARITAIN ON
THE CAUSE OF EVIL

Maritain, quoting two very important texts of St. Thomas in regard to the cause of evil, says:

I would like to quote to you two texts of his, which in their simplicity sovereignly command the whole question, and which we should inscribe on our walls; let us call them our two most sacred axioms:

First axiom: *Deus nullo modo est causa peccati, neque directe, neque indirecte* (God is absolutely not the cause of moral evil, neither directly nor indirectly). You notice the import of these words *"nullo modo,"* absolutely not, and *"neque directe, neque indirecte,"* neither directly nor indirectly. Every shadow of indirect causality must be excluded.

Second axiom: *Defectus gratiae prima causa est ex nobis* (the first cause—he says indeed, the *first* cause—of the absence of grace comes from us). It is in us, it is in the creature that the first cause of moral evil (first cause in the order of non-being or of nothingness) is to be found. The creature has the first initiative of moral evil; it is in the creature that the *initiative* and the *invention* of sin have their origin.

Here we have the two texts which command everything. The second one (the first cause of the absence of grace comes from us) had been enunciated at greater length by St. Thomas in his *Commentary on the Sentences*, I, dist. 40, q. 4, a. 2: "It is...evident that the first cause of the absence of grace is purely and simply on the side of the man to whom grace is lacking (because he has not been willing to receive it)."[15]

In Chapter II of *God and the Permission of Evil*,[16] Maritain returns to the fundamental positions of *Existence and the Existent*.[17]

Basing himself on the principle that distinguishes the dependence of the "ruled" on the "ruler" and the "measured" on the "measurer," and presupposing, now, the conclusion that the willful non-use of the ruler (God's law and man's reason as it is related to God's law), he says:

The leading idea of *Existence and the Existent* is very simple. It is a question of following through to the end that dissymmetry between the line of good and the line of evil on which I have already insisted so much; and consequently of recognizing all the bearing of this assertion that the *first cause* or the inventor of moral evil in the existential reality of the world is the liberty of the creature—I mean, this liberty in the line of non-being. All of this implies that at the very first origin of the evil act—and, above all, of the evil election, which takes place in the depths of the heart—there is *not only* the fallibility of the creature, but an actual failure of the creature, a created initiative which—*since it is not caused by God*—can only be an initiative of non-being, of deficiency in being, of lack, what I have called nihilation.[18]

The reader will do well to substitute "privation," "deprivation," etc., for "non-being," "deficiency in being," and "lack," etc., and to apply all of these to the privation, deprivation, non-being, lack, etc., of the crooked line that is always the result of a willful refusal to use the prerequisite "ruler" to bring into being the straightness that properly identifies the straight line.

Thus:

> At bottom the whole affair is contained in the Gospel saying: Sine me nihil potestis facere, it is said in St. John, 15:5.
>
> Well, this text can be read in two ways.
>
> It can be read: Without Me you can do nothing—nothing good. This is the line of being or of good, where God has the first initiative.
>
> And it can also be read: Without Me you can do *nothingness*, without Me you can *introduce into being* that nothingness or that non-being of the due good, that privation, which is evil. And this even, this

initiative of evil, you can have it *only* without Me (for with Me it is good only that you can do).[19]

When comparing *good* and *evil* Maritain clearly writes:

> *Ens et bonum convertuntur.* The good is being, and plenitude or completion of being. When we reason in the line of good, we reason in the line of being, of that which exercises being or bears being to its accomplishment.
>
> Evil, on the contrary, of itself or insofar as evil, is absence of being, *privation* of being or of good. It is a nothingness which corrodes being. When we reason in the line of evil, we reason in the line of non-being, for evil is in nowise being; evil is only a vacuum or a lack of being, a nothingness and a privation.[20]

He continues:

> Now we know that our human intellect can conceive non-being, and therefore evil, only *ad instar entis*, after the fashion of being, and consequently by speaking of it as of *some thing*, as of a kind of so-called quality.[21]

Maritain still affirms:

> It is a radical mistake to make use, in order to explain things in the line of evil, of

types of explanation by which we explain and must explain things in the line of good.

Let me give a first example: in the line of good, God is the first and transcendent cause of our liberty and of our free decisions, so that the free act is wholly from God as first cause and wholly from us as second cause; because there is not a fibril of being which escapes the causality of God. Our liberty has the initiative of our acts, but this is a second initiative; it is God who has the first initiative. Yes, this is true for good acts; but for evil acts, or more exactly for the evil itself which vitiates these acts, it is just the contrary: in the line of evil we have our two very sacred axioms which I unite in one same statement: God is absolutely not the cause of the evil of our free acts; it is man who is the *first cause* and who has the *first initiative* of moral evil.[22]

And he concludes:

In reality, all that I do which is good comes from God and all that I do which is evil comes from me, because God has the first initiative in the line of being and because I have the first initiative in the line of non-being.

If I do the good, it is because God has moved my will from end to end, without my having taken any initiative of nothingness which would have shattered His motion at the stage where it was shatterable. All the good that I do comes from God.

If I do evil, it is because I have myself taken a first initiative to shatter, by nihilating, the shatterable motion by which God inclined me to the good, and to introduce into my acts the nothingness which vitiates them. All the evil that I do comes from me.[23]

MARITAIN AND SAINT THOMAS

Having identified the first actor, the human person, in the line of evil, Maritain turns his attention to St. Thomas and the corollary problem of the "non-consideration of the rule" as this is related to the evil act as such.

There is in the first place the theory of St. Thomas on the non-consideration of the rule. This theory is a metaphysical discovery of first importance, an absolutely fundamental one and one without which no philosophy of evil is possible....

I have tried to summarize this theory in the chapter "St. Thomas Aquinas and the Problem of Evil" of my book *De Bergson à Thomas d'Aquin*. The *cause* of evil in action is *always* a lack or a failure, a *defectus in being* or in the operative failure of the agent....

If it is a case now of the evil of action of free will, the defectus in question must itself, clearly, be *voluntary and free*. And yet on the other hand it must *not already be* an evil of free action, for then we would be in a vicious circle, and would be assigning, as cause of a certain effect (that is, of moral evil), this effect itself. We would be arguing in a circle.

Well, says St. Thomas, we must posit at the origin of moral evil, *as cause of it*, a voluntary and free defectus which itself is not yet an evil or a privation, but which is a mera negatio, a mere withdrawal from being, a mere lack of a being or a good which is not due: a mere absence which I introduce voluntarily into being.[24]

...This defectus, this free failure which is the cause of moral evil *without being itself an evil*, is the non-consideration of the rule—which is not, note well, an act of non-consideration, but a non-act of consideration. To consider the rule *is not, of itself, something due*. That a craftsman not hold his ruler in hand—this is *not*, of itself, an evil. But it is the cause in virtue of which he will saw a piece of wood wrongly. And this very fact, *not having* his ruler in hand, becomes an evil, or a privation of a due good, in the *application* to the act or the operation itself, in the very act of cutting the wood.[25]

As Maritain himself says, these are hard Thomistic positions.[26] It is precisely for this reason that these positions must be understood and must be restated in the precise way that Maritain, following Saint Thomas, has stated them.

Coming, therefore, to the very heart of the matter which considers not only the cause of evil (the initiator person) but the very act which brings into existence the evil, Maritain says:

> Note well that this non-consideration of the rule is something *real*, since it is the *cause* of the sin; and it is something *free*, it is therefore a free initiative of the will. And it is the *cause* of the evil of the act of choice only according as the act of choice takes place at an instant of time when it is present. And yet, being *cause* of the evil, it *precedes* the evil, at least by a priority of nature.[27]

SAINT THOMAS ON THE CAUSE OF EVIL

Maritain, in the *Problem of Evil*, returns to the same subject of the relationship of the human person to the injection of evil, this time by a direct approach to the sources in St. Thomas himself. His concern is to further identify the defect itself in the busy or the active powers of the agent, what is in the will itself, and the exact relationship of this defect to the evil act itself. His concern, too, is to show that St. Thomas himself asks and responds to

> what is that failure in being which is the metaphysical *root* of evil action and which is itself free without being already an evil?
>
> Let us read what St. Thomas himself says on the subject in the *Quaestiones Disputatae de Malo*. Here one must, he explains, "preconsider a certain defect in the will, a certain deficiency prior to the act of choice which is itself deficient."[28]

It is here that Maritain identifies Saint Thomas himself as the author of the principle, emphasized above and throughout this study, that wherever there is a relationship between the ruler and the ruled or the measure and the measured, the "good" of the ruled or the measured, resides in the good of the ruler or the measurer. On the contrary, the evil arises from not being ruled or measured in accordance with the ruler or the measurer.

"Suppose we take a craftsman who must cut wood in a straight line according to a certain ruler: if he does not cut it in a straight line, that is, if he makes a bad cutting, that bad cutting *will be caused* by the fact that the craftsman *did not hold the ruler in his hand*. Similarly, delectation and everything that happens in human affairs should be measured and ruled according to the rule of reason and of divine law. That the will *does not use* (let us take careful note of the simple negation expressed here) —that the will does not make use of the rule of reason and of divine law," that it does not have the ruler in its hand,—*this then*, is the absence or the deficiency "which must be considered in the will before the *faulty choice* in which alone moral evil consists. And for that very absence or that lack which consists in not making use of the rule," not taking the rule in hand, "there is no need to seek a cause, for the very freedom of will, whereby it can act or not act, is enough." The lack or defect which we are discussing has as its primary cause freedom itself, which can act or not act and which does not act, does not pay attention to the rule; and this defect comes, I do not mean in time but in ontological order, before the act of choice. Here we are at the very beginning; impossible to go any further back: a *free defect*, a defect of which freedom itself is the negative and deficient primary cause;—and it is the will *thus in default which, acting with this defect*, is the cause—in quantum deficiens— of moral evil.[29]

3

God Knows Evil
Why Does He Permit It?

HOW IS EVIL KNOWN BY GOD?

"God knows evil, to be sure," states Maritain, "and He knows it perfectly, *through the good* of which evil is the privation."[1]

Then, in Chapter III of the same text, "How Is Evil Known by God?", he takes up in detail this difficult question. To reach the resolution, he begins by identifying the principles which must be applied. They include the incontrovertible fact that God cannot be the cause of evil; that, because of this, God must know evil without having caused it, that God knows "other things" than Himself in His essence; that God's "science of vision," which is par excellence a science of presentness, descends even to things in their singularity and in their contingent existence; that God attains to things fully and existentially, because of His creative action in their regard; that all changes in things remain on the side of things only; and, that, therefore, the negation that is related to the non-consideration of the rule by the human person is the key to the resolution of this question as it is the explanation of will in the human person.[2]

In his treatment, Maritain continues his reliance on St. Thomas:

> ...It is thus that the 'science of vision,' which knows all that it knows in the uncreated essence and the uncreated light, descends even to the created existent taken in its created existentiality and its created activity themselves and as such, knows it according to the very existence which it has *extra Deum:* just as, to employ St. Thomas' comparison, "through the *species* of the stone that the eye has within it, the eye knows the stone *secundum esse quod habet extra oculum,* according to the existence that it has outside the eye."[3]

Confessing his weakness in meeting with the difficulty of the question, Maritain continues:

> This is how...God knows in its presentness the human clay which His hands shape, knows it even to the most hidden core of itself and of its contingent and free activity, right down to the last depths and to the slightest tremblings of its subjectivity.[4]

But how does God know the free *privation* which is the *evil of the sinful act?* Created liberty, in fact, has need only of itself to omit to consider God's rule and thus introduce into its action the *nothingness* or absence of due good. Maritain asks this same question and answers:

> And now, what is the case with the line of non-being when non-being comes— *mere negation* as the free non-consideration of the rule or *privation* as evil—when non-being comes to fissure this clay through the deficient or nihilating first initiative of created liberty?
>
> Let us first consider the case of the free non-consideration of the rule. And let us understand well that this free non-consideration [of the rule] is neither a being nor an act but a non-act and a non-being, a mere

absence, a vacuum—and a vacuum produced not in a specifying object, but in a simple term materially attained which is known by the divine science without determining it in the least. It suffices that the divine science know *perfectly* and existentially this term materially attained, for it *at the same stroke* to know *in it*, in it which it invests on all sides, the lack which at such or such moment of time comes to it from its created liberty. Not the slightest determination of the divine knowledge by anything created is implied here....

. . . .

This culpable nihilation is known *in the created existent itself*, in the *terminus materialiter attactus*, from the very fact that the 'science of vision' which invests the latter in its entirety, even to the deepest strata of what its concrete singularity is and is not at each moment of time, knows it *perfectly* and *existentially*.

What is this to say? I recalled a moment ago that created things, which are for the divine knowledge but a "term materially attained," are for it *effects* rather than *objects*, in other words are constituted or caused *existing* and constituted or caused *known* by the 'science of vision'—and enter thus as a pure gratuitous surplus into the immutable and eternal knowledge which God has of Himself. Well, it is the 'ter-

minus materialiter attactus' in its existential integrity, with all its being and all its non-being, which is thus constituted or caused *known*. It is only according to its being that it is constituted or caused *existing*, but it is according to its being *and its non-being* (according to all the positive that it does through its second initiative, but also according to the nothingness—*mera negatio* and *privation*—that it "does" through its first initiative) that it is constituted or caused *known* by the 'science of vision.' And this is not surprising since non-being obviously cannot *exist* but can *be known* (*in* the being in which it is a lack and *through* the being whose negation or privation it is).[5]

Maritain admits that he is speaking of things entirely above our comprehension, but he concludes over and over again: "God knows moral evil through the created existents whom He knows through His essence and through His creative ideas."[6]

St. Thomas himself teaches the same when he says: "God knows evil *through the things that He causes to exist* and which themselves He knows in knowing His essence and not that God knows evil through alleged antecedent permissive decrees!"[7]

IF GOD KNOWS EVIL, WHY DOES HE PERMIT IT?

Maritain says that God, who is the transcendent First Cause, is more really and more perfectly Cause because He Himself confers on created things, which are nothing over against Him, the power themselves also to cause.

Thus, God permits the existents, whom He has Himself endowed with intelligence and free will, to collaborate in His eternal purpose of good. However, one could say, that, because of this, the work of God runs risks, risks that are *real* because the free creature can introduce evil. In this regard Maritain explains:

> All right! It is indeed true that in this view the Creator of the world does not provide Himself with the absolutely safe spectacle of a game of marionettes which would but put into execution a program that He Himself has conceived for evil as well as for good. It is indeed true that in this view, if God wills that we engage ourselves headlong in the battle, it is because He Himself has first engaged in it the glory of His name, nay more, because He has engaged Himself in it completely, by sending us His Son, one with Him in nature.

In this view, the creature, each time that it does evil, introduces to this extent nothingness into being, and undoes for a part the work that God makes. The work of God runs risks, risks that are real because the drama is not merely portrayed, it is actually *lived*. They are abysses which open out, collapses, disasters. The gods from below that free agents are when they take the initiative of nothingness, cause evil and perversion to multiply, and invent forms of horror and of abomination which astonish the angels (and, if I may say so, be it only to tease a little my neo-Banezian friends, astonish the Author Himself of the drama, in this sense that if He knows in His "science of simple intelligence" all *possible* evil, it is not He, it is the creature who invents *existing* evil, and in such an invention goes beyond all expectation).

But it is in all this, exactly, that the invincible wisdom and the dazzling power of the eternal purposes manifest themselves. He whose Name is above every name, the eternally Victorious is certain to win the game finally; He wins it at each instant, even when He seems to be losing it. Each time that a free creature undoes for its part the work that God makes, God remakes to that extent—for the better—this work and leads it to higher ends. Because of the presence of evil on earth, everything on earth, from the beginning to the end of time, is in perpetual recasting. However real the risks may be, much more real still is the strength of the arm which causes them to be surmounted by creation and repairs the damages incurred by the latter. However deep the abysses may be, however great the collapses and the disasters, sublimer are the heights and the goods to which created being will be transferred. And doubtless there will also be, finally, real losses—all too real—but themselves compensated by the manifestation of eternal justice in the creature when, in order to remain to itself its ultimate End, it prefers over love all the pains of Hell. And the more the gods from below cause horror and evil to multiply, the more the saints in their love, accomplishing in their flesh what is lacking to the sufferings of Christ, cause the magnificence of good to superabound.... And finally it is by having made good use of his liberty moved and activated from end to end by God, and by having from all eternity contributed for his part as free second cause to the very establishment of the eternal plan, that the creature saved—the one who in the end will not have said *No*—will enter into the glory that God has prepared for those who love Him, and which was His intention in creating the world, this world where evil is permitted.[8]

At this point Maritain quotes a text of St. Paul referring to the infinite goodness of God: "...however great the number of sins committed, grace was even greater."[9] Then, he also quotes this text of St. Augustine: "God would never permit evil if He was not strong enough and good enough to draw good even from evil."[10] Maritain comments:

The greater good of which St. Augustine speaks—it is in the order of the goods of grace that we have considered it, and rightly so. For it is there that is found the greater good *par excellence*—the only one which can give the final answer to our anxieties,—to which are ordained *absolutely speaking, simpliciter*, all the evils that God permits, evil of fault and evil of suffering.

It is clear that this greater good *simpliciter* cannot be merely the good of the universe or of the world of nature; for if it is a question of the sin of a *person* (and even of his suffering), it is not in the perfection of the machine of the world, it is only in the goods of grace and of glory, and the person-to-person love which unites created agents with God and among themselves there where we are fellow-citizens of the saints, that these evils can be compensated and supercompensated by a good incomparably greater in the line of good than they are in the line of evil.

It is the good which has been prepared for the Jerusalem of heaven and the communion of saints, and creation completely transfigured—and for each friend of God in particular, because "to them that love God, *all things work together unto good*," says St. Paul—and in particular for the poor and the persecuted, and for the victims of crimes and abominations of which created liberty has been the nihilating first cause and the execution of which God has permitted (and even also, in a sense, for their authors, to whom the grace of repentance will be offered at any moment whatever, be it the last moment of their life.)[11]

Previously Maritain had quoted Saint Cyprian who wrote: "The adversary can do nothing against us without the prior permission of God."[12] Maritain added: "God permits evil only in view of a greater good, that is to say, by referring or ordaining this evil to a greater good."[13] He also thinks that the law of the permission of evil for a greater good applies also in the domain of temporal history:

It is verified in the law of the two-fold simultaneous progress of good and evil, of the wheat and the cockle—but progress greater in the case of good or of the wheat; for, everything considered, the good is certainly stronger than evil.

It is true that grace and nature not being two closed worlds, but two worlds open one to the other and in mutual communication, it might happen that the *greater progress* (of the wheat over that of the cockle) of which I have just spoken would occur *more* in the order of grace than in that of nature, where in that case it would be masked by the progress of the cockle. This is why we have the *duty* to *hope* for the temporal history of men, but without any certitude that the progress of evil will not there accompany, with too much power and too much glitter, the progress of good.

Let us hope (and let us do *all* that is humanly possible—in honesty of conscience—to attain this) that from social evils which revolt us, from slavery, from misery, from the power of great monsters which devour the individual person, from the barbarous conditions in which so many of God's creatures live, human history will emerge not only with the cessation of these evils, but with an increase of goods for humanity—so that the spirit may gain ascendancy, that the unification of the human race may come about under the sign of liberty, not of a herd conformism, and that all men may have access free of charge to the elementary good of human life![14]

God plays fair with His intelligent creatures. He deals with them according to their nature, that is, as free beings. He does not want them to do evil, because He is all good, but He permits them to do it, to leave them free. However, His will of doing good never changes:

> ...if they are free beings, according to the proper, and therefore fallible, mode of their liberty,...He permits that they fail. From the moment that created persons are naturally peccable, there will be some who will in fact sin; and even, if it is a question of human beings after original sin, all will sin to some extent or other, except in Heaven (and excepting Jesus—whose person is divine—and His Mother). Hence we must conclude that in fact God would not have created nature if He had not ordained it to grace and to that charity by which man becomes, under grace, freely the friend of God; and that sin is the ransom of glory.[15]

It is so true that God can and always will work good out of evil, that Maritain dares to state: "No martyr without some executioner."[16] And he adds immediately:

The Word was made flesh in order to redeem the world by His sacrifice and His immolation, and this presupposes murderers.

On the side of the eternal purposes this supreme act of love and obedience that is the immolation of Christ according as it is accepted and willed by Him, and the infinite merits with which it is resplendent, and the redemptions that it effects—all the good, at once human and divine, of this immolation is *willed* by God. But He wills all this good without willing in any way, either directly or indirectly, the sin committed by the authors of the death of Jesus. This sin remains absolutely outside the field of divine causation—God is absolutely not the cause of it, even the cause *per accidens*.

. . . .

...If it is a question of the sin of a particular individual such as Judas, for example, then no man in the world, even supposing that he knew perfectly the character of Judas, and the circumstances, could be *certain* that he would betray Jesus. It is on an initiative of nothingness (non-consideration of the rule) of which created liberty, which escapes all necessitation of whatever sort, takes or does not take the first initiative, that this sin depends.... It was therefore possible, absolutely speaking, that Judas not betray his Master.[17]

If the events which took place in the Passion and death of Jesus appear as something necessary, inevitable, immutably established in the Passion of Jesus, it is because they actually occurred due to the free will of the murderers:

> The fact remains that such is the case because things happened in this manner, but that this was not *necessary* (except on the side of the eternal plan and hypothetically, *once supposed* the eternal purposes which, account being taken of the nihilatings of created liberty, have immutably established that things would happen in this manner—and which themselves, absolutely speaking, could have been different).[18]

PREDESTINATION AND REPROBATION

It has been demonstrated that God is most innocent in the matter of moral evils, such as violence, injustice, and wars spread all over the world, and in the matter of such depressing problems as abortion, divorce, pornography, sexism, alcoholism, drugs, vandalism, crimes, greed, lack of respect for human life in all its aspects, etc. All such evils depend on the voluntary free will of human creatures.

Now it is necessary to see, at least very briefly,[19] what the mystery of "Predestination" and "Reprobation" really mean. To explain this, Maritain makes a distinction:

I am speaking of the distinction, in God, between the will called *antecedent* and the will called *consequent*; better to say, doubtless: primordial or 'uncircumstanced' will, on the one hand; and, on the other, definitive or *circumstanced* will.

It is the consequent or circumstanced will which is always accomplished, whether it be will to do or will to permit. It is the *absolute* will of God.

But the primordial or uncircumstanced will, the antecedent will, by which God wills that "all men be saved and come to the Knowledge of the truth"—St. Paul says expressly, that *all* men be *saved*, that *all* men come to the knowledge of the truth—this will is nevertheless very *real*, although *conditional*. It is not a simple velleity, a barely outlined movement by which one does not *will* something but only *would will* it (although St. Thomas did on one occasion employ rather untowardly the word *velleitas*, but not in this sense). St. Thomas does not say that God would like or prefer, or that He has a vague and hesitant desire; he says that God *wills* that all men be saved. The uncircumstanced will is a *formal* and properly so-called will (see, on this point, John of Saint-Thomas, *Cursus Theologicus*, t. III, disp. 5, art. 7 and 8). It is the first root of the whole divine economy. But this primordial will of the infinite Goodness, by which, taking account only of itself and leaving aside every other consideration, it wills that all our acts be good and that we be saved, is a *conditional* will, and it can be frustrated. Frustrated how? by what sorts of "circumstances"?—By the initiatives of nothingness of that created liberty which God Himself has made and which He has Himself decided to leave a clear field in governing the world.

When on the contrary, it is not frustrated by a free initiative of nothingness of the creature, then, as I put it in *Existence and the Existent*, the antecedent will is *confirmed* by the *consequent* will. I have never said nor thought that it would *realize*; it is clear that as soon as there is realization there is consequent or absolute will. But when this realization is something good and in the very measure in which it is something good, a good and meritorious act especially, it is obviously willed *both* by the antecedent will and the consequent will (which have in this case a same object).

Each time that by God's consequent or circumstanced absolute will a shatterable motion to good is given to a creature, the antecedent or uncircumcised will is therein confirmed by the consequent will; and each time that this shatterable motion, not having been shattered, fructifies into an unshatterable motion to which it gives way, the antecedent will is therein confirmed by the consequent will. Each time that man does the good, it is not only the consequent will, it is also the antecedent will of God that is done on earth—as confirmed then by the consequent will. Each time that a soul is saved, the antecedent will, which wills that *all* souls be saved, is obviously accomplished—as confirmed by the consequent will.[20]

Returning to the meaning of "predestination" and "reprobation," Maritain starts by rejecting the *unconditioned positive reprobation*, that is, the predestination of souls to the eternal punishment of hell, without consideration of their future sins. This would lead to a denial of the universality of the divine will for salvation, and of the redemption, and would contradict the justice and holiness of God, as well as the freedom of man.

Then Maritain explains.

What, then, is the solution? Well, we know that by His primordial or antecedent will God wills that all men be saved—He wills that all be saved *if only* they do not refuse, for all this is an affair of love, and love necessarily implies liberty and free gift. He wills that all be saved *if only* certain ones do not frustrate this antecedent will of universal salvation by a free nihilating of their will which will make them, at the very instant when it settles down for eternity, prefer to the beatific vision and to the love of God over and above all, the love over and above all of their own grandeur, be it at the price of all the flames and gnashings of teeth.[21]

What does this mean? Here, Maritain uses a beautiful, moving and convincing comparison:

"I choose all," said the little Theresa of Lisieux. Cannot God do the same? And this is where the analogical concept of choice is properly elaborated.

By His antecedent will God *chooses them all* (conditionally); by His antecedent will they are, with a total gratuitousness, *all chosen* (conditionally, since to be conditional or uncircumstanced is the proper characteristic of the antecedent will).[22]

PREDESTINATION

At this point one comes in contact with the mystery, which, however, does not annul the universality of the divine will for salvation:

> Now it goes without saying that God can give to certain ones *motions unshatterable from the very first*. Their liberty will be, to this extent, divinely preserved from its natural fallibility, will act well without running the risk of failing, will be divinely protected against the eventuality of a non-consideration of the rule. But it is clear also that this is not the ordinary case, since, as I have just noted, it is a general law that God deals with us according to the mode of our nature. A motion *unshatterable from the very first* is something extraordinary, exceptional supra-human; God gives such motions at His pleasure, to be sure, to whomever He wills in whatever cases He wills. This is the mystery of the divine free predilections.[23]

None is excluded, says Maritain, but each has been conditionally chosen:

> But ordinarily, normally, according to the fallible mode called for by our fallible nature, what God gives to free agents is

shatterable motions, which are shattered if at the moment of time when the election is about to be made the free agent nihilates in not considering the rule; and which, if they *are not* thus shattered, fructify *of themselves*, I say of themselves or by the very love of God from which they proceed, of God Who has loved us first—fructify of themselves, without having need of being completed by the slightest actuation of determination coming from the creature, into unshatterable motions (let us say, if you will, into efficacious graces) which replace them and under which the creature, freely and fallibly, will consider the rule in its very operation and will produce the good act to which it is moved by God.[24]

In the following, Maritain insists on the truth already taught, that, while a person can do evil by himself, he needs God's grace to do good:

And if you have well understood all this, you have understood also that it is *ante praevisa merita*, anteriorly to any merit on their part, by reason only of the pure initiative of the divine goodness, by reason only of the creative and saving love which is directed on them, that *all* the elect are chosen and predestined, those who are chosen unconditionally from the very first, and those who are chosen unconditionally from the fact that a voluntary nihilating of created liberty *has not* frustrated the antecedent divine will. No one 'discerns himself' for, or makes himself worthy of, eternal life; it is an absolutely free gift of the grace and generosity of God. The merits of the elect, far from being the reason of their election, are there, on the contrary, because from all eternity ("before the world was")—in that eternity to which all the instants of the life of a man, the last as well as the first, are present together —the elect have been unconditionally chosen by the absolute will of God, either at one stroke, or, if it is a question of the "general run of the elect," according as it confirms the antecedent will, this latter not having been frustrated.[25]

In regard to this last affirmation, Maritain explains that God is always the one who has the first initiative in doing good:

In the line of good it is God who has the first initiative and who causes absolutely everything as first cause. And in this line of good the initiative of creatures— although essentially dependent and second—has a value and an efficacy certainly much greater than in the line of evil, since the good is being. "When the disciples," writes Monsignor Journet, "asked Christ to teach them to pray, he gave them the Lord's Prayer, and the first three paradoxical petitions that they had to address to God" for "divine things," which "therefore will come about partially in dependence on our human initiatives. It must be concluded that the fervor with which God's friends pray will decide, to a very great extent, the outpourings of God's helping graces, be they regular or miraculous, the advances made by the City of God, and any progress in the conversion of the world." And all this good—it is God who causes it to be in His work, through the motions of His goodness.[26]

REPROBATION

Regarding reprobation, Maritain speaks very clearly. He says that only those who refuse God's grace to the end of their lives go to hell:

> As to the others, the condemned, it is through their fault and *by reason of their demerits* that they will have been *less loved.* I have already noted that Saint Thomas takes great care to call them the *foreknown* (and not the "negatively condemned"!). God knows from all eternity that they will be, that they are con-

demned—but not because He would have condemned them in advance, even negatively; on the contrary it is they who have refused God. It is *post praevisa demerita*, "after" their "fore"-seen demerits, that they are condemned, because they have withdrawn from divine grace by their free initiative of nihilating first cause. In short, it is they themselves who have "discerned" or discriminated themselves for evil and for Hell, when at the end of their life they have irrevocably shattered the last grace offered. At that time they have for ever preferred their own grandeur—to be to themselves their last end—to the supernatural beatitude which presupposes the love of God over and above all. They prefer Hell even while cursing it. They have that which they willed, that which they have themselves chosen as the supreme good; they have put their beatitude in themselves and they will hold fast to it, they are fixed in aversion of God.

At the same stroke, in what concerns the divine government of beings, they have passed from the watershed of mercy to that of justice: so that it is by manifesting in them His attribute of justice—justice which, to speak the truth, is above all *patience* (what is more awesome than that patience of God which makes Him endure being eternally rejected by a creature whom He has made?)—it is by manifesting in them His eternal justice that God will draw from their fault a greater good, not for them, most certainly, but this time for the whole order of created nature and of the machine of the world, since, having refused love and rejected God, they have themselves put below this order all that which by the privileges of personality emerged in them above it.[27]

Maritain now stresses the fact that even the damned were called by God to salvation and for this they were given the graces to the end of their lives, but they despised God's mercy and chose hell by their own free will:

And let us make here one further remark. In their regard God wills the good of His justice and of their just chastisement, but because it is they who have excluded themselves from the goods to which in the first place and of Himself He had ordained them. It is not *in view* of their just chastisement, and of the manifestation of His justice, that He has permitted their sins! It is *by reason of their obstinacy in evil* that their faults serve finally the epiphany of God's justice appearing in its terrifying beauty.

All the faults that they have committed during their life, God has permitted them by referring them to a greater good, to a greater work of love—the good of the superabundance of grace, and of the reparations effected by the charity of the saints; and, as concerns the fore-known themselves, this greater good included as one of its elements—conditionally, if they did not evade the proferred grace—their repentance. And from all eternity God sees that they have so evaded. And at the end of their life the last motion which He has sent them was directed toward their final repentance, and it is they themselves who by their initiative of nothingness have shattered this motion. And all this is from all eternity naked before God, so that all this is determinately established, even to the least ripple of the water, as well as all the rest, in His eternal purposes.[28]

There are passages in Sacred Scripture which describe the hardening of the sinner, as, for example, the following: "I myself will make Pharaoh's heart stubborn,... Pharaoh will not listen to you."[29] And again: "But Yahweh made Pharaoh's heart stubborn, and, as Yahweh had foretold, he refused to listen to them."[30] Also, in Romans, the Apostle Paul says:

> ...as scripture says elsewhere: I showed my love for Jacob and my hatred for Esau.
>
> Does it follow that God is unjust? Of course not. Take what God said to Moses: I have mercy on whom I will, and I show pity to whom I please. In other words, the only thing that counts is not what human beings want or try to do, but the mercy of God.... In other words, when God wants to show mercy he does, and when he wants to harden someone's heart he does so.[31]

These and similar passages must be understood in the sense that God permits evil by withdrawing grace from the sinner as a punishment. Repentance, therefore, will be more difficult, but not impossible. Saint Augustine says: "One must not despair of even the greatest sinner as long as he lives here on earth."[32] The reason for the possibility of even the most stubborn sinner's conversion lies in the fact that the will of a person while he is still alive on this earth can change, in contrast to the immutable will of the damned in hell.[33]

Recalling here the use or non-use of the ruler, predestination takes on a significant meaning when related to the proper and improper use of the ruler of human actions. One *predestines* himself to draw the crooked line when he fails to use the ruler; and, he *predestines* himself to draw the straight line when he uses the ruler, without which he cannot draw the straight line (do the good!).

To conclude Maritain uses the very words of St. Paul and St. Thomas:

> "Deus omnipotens *omnes homines* sine exceptione *vult salvos fieri* (1 Tm. 2:4), licet non omnes salventur. Quod autem quidam salvantur, salvantis est donum; quod autem quidam pereunt, pereuntium est meritium." "Almighty God wills that all men without exception be saved, although not all may be saved. Now, that certain ones be saved, this is the gift of Him who saves; and that certain ones perish, this is the fault (meritum) of those who perish."[34]

St. Augustine himself had taught: "God is good, God is just. He can save a person without good works, because He is good; but He cannot condemn anyone without evil works, because He is just."[35]

4

Salvation in Christ Jesus

St. Augustine makes this charge against the Pelagians:

> If all the saints could be assembled on earth and asked if they were without sin, they would, with one voice, answer with the Apostle St. John (1 Jn. 1:8): If we were to say that we were without sin, then we would deceive ourselves, and the truth would not be in us.[1]

The previous three chapters have followed St. Thomas and Jacques Maritain through their philosophical-theological treatment of the problem of evil.

In this last chapter attention shall be centered on the scriptural sources which pursue man through his fall and his redemption.

The heritage of sin belongs to every man. Speaking to a general audience, Pope John Paul II said:

The tree of the knowledge of good and evil, as expression and symbol of the covenant with God broken in man's heart, delimits and contrasts two diametrically opposed situations and states: that of original innocence and that of original sin, and at the same time of man's hereditary sinfulness which is derived from it.[2]

The Pope continued:

The state of sin is part of "historical man," both of the one of whom we read in Matthew 19, that is Christ's questioner at that time [about divorce], and also of any other potential or actual questioner of all times of history, and therefore, naturally, also of modern man.[3]

Long before, the great Apostle St. Paul, in his Letter to the Romans, described the weakness of "fallen" nature by reason of concupiscence, against the assaults of temptations, and stressed the necessity of divine help in order to overcome them:

The Law, of course, as we all know, is spiritual; but I am unspiritual; I have been sold as a slave to sin. I cannot understand my own behavior. I fail to carry out the things I want to do, and I find myself doing the very things I hate. When I act against my own will, that means I have a self that acknowledges that the Law is good, and so the thing behaving in that way is not my self but sin living in me. The fact is, I know of nothing good living in me—living, that is, in my unspiritual self—for though the will to do what is good is in me, the performance is not, with the result that instead of doing the good things I want to do, I carry out the sinful things I do not want. When I act against my will, then, it is not my true self doing it, but sin which lives in me.

In fact, this seems to be the rule, that every single time I want to do good it is something evil that comes to hand. In my inmost self I dearly love God's Law, but I can see that my body follows a different law that battles against the law which my reason dictates. This is what makes me a prisoner of that law of sin which lives inside my body.

What a wretched man I am! Who will rescue me from this body doomed to death? Thanks be to God through Jesus Christ our Lord!

In short, it is I who with my reason serve the Law of God, and no less I who serve in my unspiritual self the law of sin.[4]

The cry of Paul is the cry of humanity. "The multitude of sins," in fact, states the *General Catechetical Directory*, "has become a sorrowful experience for mankind, and it is also the cause of manifold sorrows and ruin."[5] But man must not despair. From the first moment of the fall God manifested His infinite goodness and mercy toward His rational creature.

Pope John Paul II continues:

> We are witnesses of when man, male and female, after breaking the original covenant with his Creator, receives the first promise of redemption in the words of the so-called Proto-gospel in Genesis 3:15:
> "Then Yahweh God said to the serpent,
> ...'I will make you enemies of each other:
> you and the woman,
> your offspring and her offspring.
> He will crush your head
> and you will strike at his heel.' "[6]

So started the history of salvation, which is the history of liberation from sin. God willed to redeem man. When the fullness of time came, according to His promise, God sent His Son.[7] Jesus will save His people from their sins.[8] He, the Son of God, gave His life on the cross as a sacrifice for the reconciliation of all mankind, for the blotting out of human guilt, for the forgiveness of the sins of all. Thus, as all participate in the history of human sinfulness, so all participate in the history of salvation, that is, in the mystery of redemption.[9] How great is man's dignity and how precious man must be in God's eyes if the Creator sent so great a Redeemer and if God gave His only Son in order that man "may not be lost but may have eternal life"![10] "For of all the names in the world given to men, this is the only one by which we can be saved."[11] It is the name of Jesus. Repentance and the forgiveness of sins are preached in His name.[12] And through faith all have "life in his name."[13]

Sending His apostles to continue His mission of salvation, Jesus said to them: "Go, therefore, make disciples of all the nations; baptize them in the name of the Father and of the Son and of the Holy Spirit."[14]

Speaking about Baptism, John Paul II says:

On the day of our Baptism, we received the greatest gift God can bestow on any man or woman. No other honor, no other distinction will equal its value. For we were freed from sin and incorporated into Christ Jesus and His Body, the Church. That day and every day after, we were chosen "to live through love in his presence" (Eph. 1:4).[15]

In a previous address the Pope had beautifully stressed the new divine life received in Baptism, together with all the supernatural virtues and gifts. He also enumerated the evil inclinations still remaining within man due to original sin, adding that his work should be to develop the first and to combat and transform, with God's help, the latter:

> ...Knowing Christ and through Him also the Father—"He who has seen me has seen the Father" (Jn. 14:9)—we become, in the Holy Spirit, participants in the new life which Christ has grafted into us from the moment of Baptism and which He has strengthened with Confirmation.

> This new life which Christ has given us becomes our spiritual life, our interior life. We therefore discover within ourselves the interior person with its qualities, talents, worthy desires and ideals; but we also discover our weaknesses, our vices, our evil inclinations: selfishness, pride and sensuality. We perfectly understand how much the first of these aspects of our humanity needs to be developed and strengthened, and how much instead the second one must be overcome, combatted and transformed.

In this way—in living contact with Jesus, in the contact of the disciple with the Master—there begins and develops the most sublime activity of man: work on himself that aims at the formation of his own humanity.[16]

Only *when* and *if* man draws near to Christ the Redeemer, yes, even with his weaknesses and sinfulness, will he find again his human dignity, greatness and the meaning of his very life in the world.

Coming from God's hands, so as to glorify Him and be happy with Him in heaven for all eternity, man must first make a journey of trial, called life.

Three fundamental aspirations were impressed on him by his Creator, by means of which he would be guided, persuaded and spurred on toward his end: the aspiration toward happiness, which he tends to achieve through the acts of his will; the aspiration toward truth, which he tends to possess through the activity of his intellect; and the aspiration toward love, which he tends to attain through the movement of his heart.

But sin saw the spirit of rebellion in man's will, diffused ignorance and error in his intellect, and suppressed love in his heart. Therefore, man, instead of tending toward God as to his supreme end, seeks happiness in creatures and material things, thus causing a perennial restlessness in his spirit.

Yet, God wants man to be saved. He calls him to stop sinning and to reform his life. The inspired words of St. Paul, which converted St. Augustine, are also addressed to modern man:

> Let us give up all the things we prefer to do under cover of the dark; let us arm ourselves and appear in the light. Let us live decently as people do in the daytime: no drunken orgies, no promiscuity or licentiousness, and no wrangling or jealousy. Let your armor be the Lord Jesus Christ; forget about satisfying your bodies with all their cravings.[17]

This is hard work. But with God's help nothing is impossible. Jesus is man's Savior and also his Master, his Teacher. He destroyed man's sins, and He redirected man to God, to heaven: "I am," He said, "the Way, the Truth and the Life."[18]

As *Way*, He guides man's will to eternal goods and reunion with the heavenly Father; as *Truth*, He directs man's intellect to the eternal truths, which alone can answer all the questions of the human soul;

as *Life*, He re-establishes and diffuses love in man's heart by means of grace. Only after he turned to Christ could Augustine exclaim: "You made us for Yourself, O Lord, and our hearts have no peace until they rest in You." "Too late have I known You and loved You!"[19]

Through *faith* man adheres to God, the fount of truth; through *hope* he desires Him, the fount of blessedness; through *charity* he unites himself, together with Christ, to God, who is infinite love.

God's love for man did not stop at creation and redemption; it reached the farthest extreme. All of redemption, the drama of the God-man who was born, died, rose from the dead and ascended into heaven, is perpetuated, renewed and applied throughout the centuries in the inexpressible mystery of the Holy Eucharist. For this reason the Holy Eucharist is God's most precious gift to mankind. To each of the faithful who receives the Eucharist, Jesus Master repeats His divine words: "Anyone who does eat my flesh and drink my blood has eternal life, and I shall raise him up on the last day."[20] The Eucharist is truly the pledge of future glory.

In the Holy Eucharist Jesus is truly present and active. He is *present*, because in the Eucharist He lives as true God and true man, with His glorious body, soul and divinity. He is *active*, because in the Eucharist He continues His mission of mediator between God and man.

Jesus in the Holy Eucharist is the Way, Truth and Life.

He is *Way* because the memory of His passion, death and resurrection is renewed in the Mass, and in this memory and renewal of all the work of sanctification and of immolation accomplished by Jesus, there is traced out for man the way to be united to the Father. Jesus the Way repeats to everyone the words: "If anyone wants to be a follower of mine, let him renounce himself and take up his cross and follow me."[21]

He is *Truth*, because the Eucharist is a mystery of faith. At the school of Jesus Master, living in the Eucharist, one elevates himself in the meditation and contemplation of the most sublime truths and most profound mysteries of God. Thus, the mind is filled with divine light.

He is *Life*, because the Eucharist is a "sacred banquet in which Christ is received,"[22] a banquet in which Jesus gives Himself to souls without any reservation, to the consummation of charity.

The Eucharist is the redemption in action. Jesus Master, Way, Truth and Life, living and active in the Eucharist, daily makes the soul more believing in its faith, more active in its hope, more loving in its charity, up to the perfection of the Christian life and its consummation in heaven, which is eternal vision, possession and love in the one and triune God.

In all his prayers St. Thomas keeps these fruits of the Eucharist in mind. For him the Eucharist is always a banquet of faith, hope and charity. In his beautiful prayer, *Jesu, dulcissime,* he calls the Eucharist sweetness to the soul, light to the intellect, virtue for the will, health and peace for the body. In a prayer of thanksgiving after Mass, he prays that Communion will be "the armor of faith, shield of good will, firm adhesion to You, one and true God, happy consummation of my end."[23]

Jesus said: "I have come so that they may have life and have it to the full."[24] In the Eucharist Jesus comes into souls to purify them from venial sins; to strengthen them against the temptations of the flesh, the devil and the spirit of the world; to fill them with joy and energy in continuing the spiritual work and keeping God's law; and to increase the divine life and produce the most intimate union with Him.

The holy Curé of Ars says: "Make frequent Communions and make them well! You will be blessed eternally for them!"[25]

The best preparation to make fruitful Communions is the Sacrament of Penance, through which sins are forgiven and souls are strengthened with grace.

Addressing the Bishops of the United States, and speaking about the Sacrament of Penance, Pope John Paul II remarks:

> ...We ourselves are called to conversion that we may preach with convincing power the message of Jesus: "Reform your lives and believe in the Gospel" (Mk. 1:15). We have a special role to play in safeguarding the sacrament of reconciliation, so that, in fidelity to a divine precept, we and our people may experience in our innermost being that "grace has far surpassed sin" (Rom. 5:20).
>
> Conversion by its very nature is the condition for that union with God which reaches its greatest expression in the Eucharist. Our union with Christ in the Eucharist presupposes, in turn, that our hearts are set

on conversion, that they are pure. This is indeed an important part of our preaching to the people.... "The Christ who calls to the Eucharistic banquet is always the same Christ who exhorts us to penance and repeats His 'repent.' Without this constant and ever-renewed endeavor for conversion, partaking of the Eucharist would lack its full redeeming effectiveness...." In the face of a widespread phenomenon of our times, namely, that many of our people who are among the great numbers who receive Communion make little use of confession, we must emphasize Christ's basic call to conversion. We must also stress that the personal encounter with the forgiving Jesus in the sacrament of reconciliation is a divine means which keeps alive in our hearts and in our communities, a consciousness of sin in its perennial and tragic reality, and which actually brings forth, by the action of Jesus and the power of His Spirit, fruits of conversion in justice and holiness of life. By this sacrament we are renewed in fervor, strengthened in our resolves and buoyed up by divine encouragement.[26]

St. John Bosco used to say to his boys: "We do not go to Communion because we are good, we go to become good."[27] Saint Augustine, out of his own experience, ad-

vises: "Daily receive with the best disposi-
tions Him whom you so greatly need every
day."[28]

God made man for heaven, but He re-
spects his freedom. "Make us come back to
you, Yahweh, and we will come back."[29]

Life's battles are many and strong.
Man's nature is weak. Jesus' words before
dying on the cross are the only hope for
every man:

> Take this, all of you, and eat it:
> this is my body *which will be given up
> for you.*
>
> Take this, all of you, and drink from
> it:
> this is the cup of my blood,
> the blood of the new and everlasting
> covenant.
> It will *be shed for you and for all men
> so that sins may be forgiven.*[30]

When His Apostles had asked Jesus
to teach them how to pray, the Master, to
whom human weakness was too well known,
made up that unsurpassed prayer, the *Our
Father*, the last words of which are:

> ...and lead us not into temptation,
> but deliver us from evil.[31]

At Mass, after having recited together with the faithful this *Lord's Prayer*, the celebrant continues with the following supplication:

> Deliver us, Lord, *from every evil*,
> and grant us peace in our day.
> In your mercy *keep us free from sin*
> and protect us from all anxiety
> as we wait in joyful hope
> for the coming of our Savior, Jesus Christ.[32]

The coming of our Savior Jesus Christ is His second coming when the general judgment will take place. Speaking about it, St. Paul recalls the abundance of God's mercy, but he also emphasizes the duty for all to avoid sin and to be eager to do good:

> You see, God's grace has been revealed, and it has made salvation possible for the whole human race and taught us that what we have to do is to give up everything that does not lead to God, and all our worldly ambitions; we must be self-restrained and live good and religious lives here in this present world, while we are waiting in hope for the blessing which will come with the Appearing of the glory of our great God and Savior Christ Jesus. He sacrificed himself for us in order to *set us*

free from all wickedness and to *purify a people so that it could be his very own* and would have no ambition except to do good.[33]

Rightly teaches St. Augustine: "He who has created you without yourself, does not justify you without yourself. Thus He created you without your knowledge, but only with your agreement and your will does He justify you."[34]

In the problem of moral evil, God not only is not the author of it, but He is the One offended by the *free* will of His rational creature. Hence, the providence of the cross of Jesus, the instrument of our salvation and the sign of God's infinite, merciful love. Hence, the wisdom of penance, which expiates, and of a consequent revision of life, with His help.

Conclusion

The purpose of this dissertation was to present the innocence of God in regard to the problem of moral evil.

In the first three chapters catechists were offered a brief but real remedy for the contemporary flood of atheistic thinking about God with the practical value of the philosophical-theological doctrine of Aquinas-Maritain. Then, in Chapter 4, they were presented with the history of human sinfulness and the history of salvation. It is faithful catechetical instruction which forms children, youth and adults to find in Jesus Christ, God with us, the Redeemer, the infallible remedy: the *Truth* to believe in order to be free; the "Rule" to follow as one's personal *Way* of life; and the *Life* Itself which fills one with joy and strength. God's grace not only makes the holy holier, but can even change great sinners into great saints. It is the greatest convert, the Apostle Paul, who wrote to Titus:

> Remember, there was a time when we too were ignorant, disobedient, and misled and enslaved by different passions and luxuries; we lived then in wickedness and ill-will, hating each other and hateful ourselves.
>
> But when the kindness and love of God our Savior for mankind were revealed, it was not because he was concerned with any righteous actions we might have done ourselves; it was for no reason except his own compassion that he saved us, by means of the cleansing water of rebirth and by renewing us with the Holy Spirit which he has so generously poured over us through Jesus Christ our Savior. He did this so that we should be justified by his grace, to become heirs looking forward to inheriting eternal life. This is doctrine that you can rely on.[1]

Moral evil, sin, can and must be overcome in individual lives as well as in society. God's mercy toward the sinner makes this possible through the application of His superabundant redemption.

The clear and powerful words of Pope John Paul II to the young people of Ireland are in place here. They can very well be considered also by adults. Unfortunately, the temptations enumerated here by the Holy Father are a trial in modern times for all:

> ...Temptations spare no society in our age. Like so many other young people in various parts of the world, you will be told that changes must be made, that you must have more freedom, that you should be different from your parents, and that the decisions about your lives depend on you, and you alone.

> The prospect of growing economic progress, and the chance of obtaining a greater share of the goods that modern society has to offer, will appear to you as an opportunity to achieve greater freedom. The more you possess—you may be tempted to think—the more you will feel liberated from every type of confinement. In order to make more money and to possess more, in order to eliminate effort and worry, you may be tempted to take moral shortcuts where honesty, truth and work are concerned. The progress of science and technology seems inevitable and you may be enticed to look towards the technological society for the answers to all your problems.

> The lure of pleasure, to be had whenever and wherever it can be found, will be strong and it may be presented to you as part of progress towards greater autonomy

and freedom from rules. The desire to be free from external restraints may manifest itself very strongly in the sexual domain, since this is an area that is so closely tied to a human personality. The moral standards that the Church and society have held up to you for so long a time, will be presented as obsolete and a hindrance to the full development of your own personality. Mass media, entertainment, and literature will present a model for living where all too often it is every man for himself, and where the unrestrained affirmation of self leaves no room for concern for others.

You will hear people tell you that your religious practices are hopelessly out of date, that they hamper your style and your future, that with everything that social and scientific progress has to offer, you will be able to organize your own lives, and that God has played out His role. Even many religious persons will adopt such attitudes, breathing them in from the surrounding atmosphere without attending to the *practical atheism that is at their origin.*

A society that, in this way, has lost its higher religious and moral principles will become an easy prey for manipulation and for domination by the forces, which, under the pretext of greater freedom, will enslave it ever more.

Yes, dear young people, do not close your eyes to the moral sickness that stalks your society today, and from which your youth alone will not protect you. How many young people have already warped their consciences and have substituted the true joy of life with drugs, sex, alcohol, vandalism and the empty pursuit of mere material possessions.[2]

These negative aspects of life today reflect the reality of moral evil. The Pope then turns to the positive aspects of salvation in Christ Jesus and concludes thus:

Something else is needed: something that you will find only in Christ, for He alone is the measure and the scale that you must use to evaluate your own life. In Christ you will discover the true greatness of your own humanity; He will make you understand your own dignity as human beings "created to the image and likeness of God" (Gen. 1:26). Christ has the answers to your questions and the key to history; He has the power to uplift hearts. He keeps calling you, He keeps inviting you, He who is "the way, and the truth, and the life" (Jn. 14:6). Yes, Christ calls you, but He calls you in truth. His call is demanding, because He invites you to let yourselves be "captured" by Him completely, so that your whole lives will be seen in a different light. He is the Son of God, who reveals to you the loving face of the Father. He is the Teacher, the only one whose teaching does not pass away, the only one who teaches with authority. He is the friend who said to His disciples, "No longer do I call you servants...but I have called you friends" (Jn. 15:15). And He proved His friendship by laying down His life for you.

His call is demanding for He taught us what it means to be truly human. Without heeding the call of Jesus, it will not be possible to realize the fullness of your own humanity. You must build on the foundation which is Christ (cf. 1 Cor. 3:11); only with Him your life will be meaningful and worthwhile.[3]

FOOTNOTES

INTRODUCTION

1. Vatican II, *Gaudium et Spes:* "The Pastoral Constitution on the Church in the Modern World," in *The Sixteen Documents of Vatican II* (Boston: St. Paul Editions), no. 19.

2. Ibid.

3. Jacques Maritain, *God and the Permission of Evil*, trans. Joseph W. Evans (Milwaukee: The Bruce Publishing Co., 1966), p. 3.

4. For *evil of nature* or *suffering*, see Appendix.

5. See *Summa Theologiae*, I, 15, 3, ad 1, cited by Maritain, *God and the Permission of Evil*, p. 112.

6. Matthew 16:27. Translations of the Bible unless otherwise noted are taken from *The Jerusalem Bible* (Garden City, N.Y.: Doubleday & Company, Inc., 1966).

7. Romans 8:28. This text is taken from *The Holy Bible*, Confraternity Edition (Boston: St. Paul Editions, 1955).

8. *Catechesi Tradendae:* "Apostolic Exhortation on Catechesis in Our Time," October 16, 1979 (Boston: St. Paul Editions, 1979), ch. 3, no. 19.

9. Ibid., ch. 4, no. 30. See also Vatican II, *Optatam Totius*, in *The Sixteen Documents of Vatican II*, nos. 15 and 16 regarding philosophy, theology and Scripture.

CHAPTER ONE

1. Jacques Maritain, *On the Philosophy of History*, trans. Joseph W. Evans (Clifton, New Jersey: Augustus M. Kelly, Publishers, 1973), pp. 123-124.

2. Ibid., p. 125.
3. Ibid., pp. 125-126.
4. Ibid., p. 126.

5. St. Thomas Aquinas, *Summa Contra Gentiles:* "On the Truth of the Catholic Faith," Book 1, trans. by Anton C. Pegis; Book 3, trans. Vernon J. Bourke (New York: Image Books, 1956), bk. 3, ch. 111, p. 114.

6. Ibid., ch. 112, p. 116.
7. Ibid., ch. 112, p. 115.
8. Ibid., p. 117.
9. Ibid., p. 116.
10. Ibid.
11. Ibid., ch. 113, p. 122.
12. Ibid., p. 121.
13. Ibid., pp. 121-122.
14. Ibid., ch. 114, pp. 122-123, 124.
15. Ibid., ch. 116, pp. 125-126.
16. Ibid., p. 126.
17. Ibid., ch. 37, p. 125.
18. Ibid., ch. 115, pp. 124, 125.
19. Ibid., bk. 1, ch. 37, p. 152; see Psalm 72:1.
20. Ibid., bk. 3, ch. 117, p. 127.
21. Ibid., pp. 127-128.
22. Ibid., p. 128.
23. Ibid.

CHAPTER TWO

1. John 1:18.

2. 2 Corinthians 5:19.

3. Genesis 1:3, 6, 9; (see also vv. 12, 18, 21, 25); 1:26, 27, 31. (Italics mine.)

4. Genesis 2:16-17; 3:1-6, 8-9, 11-14, 16-24.

5. *Gaudium et Spes*, op. cit., no. 13.

6. Genesis 6:5-14, 17-18, 19.

7. Cf. St. Thomas Aquinas, *Summa Theologiae*, ed. Blackfriars, 60 vols. (New York: McGraw-Hill Book Company, 1963), I, q. 49, 1, ad 3; cf. also Jacques Maritain, *St. Thomas and the Problem of Evil* (Milwaukee: Marquette University Press, 1942), pp. 20-38; cf. also Maritain, *God and the Permission of Evil*, pp. 23, 49, 52.

8. Maritain, *St. Thomas and the Problem of Evil*, p. 1; cf. *Summa Theologiae*, I, q. 48, 1; see *de Malo*, 1, 1; *Summa Contra Gentiles*, bk. 3, chps. 7, 8, and 9.

9. Maritain, *St. Thomas and the Problem of Evil*, p. 2.

10. Ibid., pp. 2-3.

11. Ibid., pp. 3-4.

12. *Sum. theol.*, I, q. 48, 1, 2.

13. Ibid., a. 5.

14. Ibid., a. 2.

15. Maritain, *God and the Permission of Evil*, p. 6.

16. Pages 32-66.

17. Jacques Maritain, *Existence and the Existent*, trans. Lewis Galantiere and Gerald B. Phelan (Garden City: Image Books, 1956).

18. Maritain, *God and the Permission of Evil*, p. 33. (Italics mine.)

19. Ibid. (Italics mine.)

20. Ibid., p. 9.

21. Ibid., p. 36.

22. Ibid., p. 10.

23. Ibid., pp. 41-42.

24. In this case, as it is throughout the Maritain treatment, the context adheres strictly to the related passages of St. Thomas. Cf. *De Malo*, q. 1, a. 3, corp. and ad 13; *Sum. theol.*, I, q. 49, 1, ad 3; I-II, q. 75, 1, ad 3; *Sum. contra Gent.*, bk. 3, ch. 10.

25. Maritain, *God and the Permission of Evil*, pp. 34-35. (Italics mine.)

26. Ibid., see page 32.

27. Ibid., p. 35.

28. Maritain, *St. Thomas and the Problem of Evil*, p. 24.

29. Ibid., pp. 24-25. (Italics mine.)

CHAPTER THREE

1. Maritain, *God and the Permission of Evil*, p. 5.

2. Ibid., see pp. 67-73.

3. Ibid., p. 72.

4. Ibid., p. 73.

5. Ibid., pp. 73, 74-75.

6. Ibid., p. 75.

7. *I Sent.*, dist. 36, q. 1, a. 2, cited by Maritain, *God and the Permission of Evil*, p. 75.

8. Maritain, *God and the Permission of Evil*, pp. 85-87.

9. Romans 5:20.

10. *Enchir.* III, 11, P.L., 40, 236, cited by Maritain, *God and the Permission of Evil*, p. 87.

11. Maritain, *God and the Permission of Evil*, pp. 87-88.

12. *De Orat. domin.*, n. 25, P.L., 4, 536, cited by Maritain, *God and the Permission of Evil*, p. 62.

13. Maritain, *God and the Permission of Evil*, p. 62.

14. Ibid., p. 89.

15. Ibid., pp. 37-38.

16. Ibid., p. 96.

17. Ibid., pp. 96, 97.

18. Ibid., p. 98.

19. Cf. Ludwig Ott, *Fundamentals of Catholic Dogma*, ed. James Canon Bastible (Rockford, Illinois: Tan Books and Publishers, Inc., 1974), pp. 242-245.

20. Maritain, *God and the Permission of Evil*, pp. 99-101.

21. Ibid., p. 104.

22. Ibid.

23. Ibid., pp. 38-39.

24. Ibid., p. 39.

25. Ibid., p. 106.

26. Ibid., p. 83.

27. Ibid., pp. 109-110.

28. Ibid., pp. 110-111.

29. Exodus 7:3, 4.

30. Exodus 9:12.

31. Romans 9:13-16, 18.

32. *Retract.* I, 19, 7, cited by Ott, *Fundamentals of Catholic Dogma*, p. 241.

33. Cf. Maritain, *God and the Permission of Evil*, pp. 7-8; cf. also Ott, *Fundamentals of Catholic Dogma*, pp. 240-241.

34. Maritain, *God and the Permission of Evil*, pp. 111-112; cf. *Enchiridion Symbolorum*, ed. Henricus Denzinger and Adolfus Schönmetzer, S.I. (Barcelona: Herder, 1963), DS 623 (D 318), p. 208.

35. *Contra Jul.* III, 18, 35, cited by Ott, *Fundamentals of Catholic Dogma*, p. 245.

CHAPTER FOUR

1. De nat. et grat. 36, 42, cited in *Basic Writings of St. Augustine*, ed. Whitney J. Oates (New York: Random House, 1948), vol. one.

2. John Paul II, General Audience, September 26, 1979, *L'Osservatore Romano* (English edition), no. 40 (601) October 1, 1979, p. 1.

3. Ibid.

4. Romans 7:14-25.

5. Sacred Congregation for the Clergy, *General Catechetical Directory* (Washington, D.C.: USCC Publications Office, 1971), no. 62, p. 49.

6. John Paul II, Address of September 26, 1979, *op. cit.*, p. 1.

7. See Galatians 4:4.

8. See Matthew 1:21.

9. See Romans 5:18.

10. John 3:16.

11. Acts 4:12.

12. See Luke 24:27.

13. John 20:31.

14. Matthew 28:19.

15. John Paul II, Address to Women Religious of October 7, 1979, in *U.S.A.—The Message of Justice,*

Peace and Love (Boston: St. Paul Editions, 1979), p. 243.

16. John Paul II, Address to Religious Seminarians and Novices at Jasna Gora, June 6, 1979, in *"You Are the Future, You Are My Hope"* (Boston: St. Paul Editions, 1979), pp. 212-213.

17. Romans 13:12-14.

18. John 14:6. Cf. Leo XIII, *Tametsi futura*, ASS, 33, 339, pp. 273-285; cf. also James Alberione, "Verso Un' Enciclopedia su Gesú Maestro," in *Carissimi in San Paolo*, ed. Rosario F. Esposito (Rome: Edizioni Paoline, 1971), pp. 1195-1254.

19. Confessions, bk. 1, ch. 1; bk. 10, ch. 27, in *Basic Writings of St. Augustine*.

20. John 6:54.

21. Matthew 16:24.

22. Vatican II, *Sacrosanctum Concilium:* The Constitution on the Sacred Liturgy, in *The Sixteen Documents of Vatican II*, no. 47.

23. *Vatican II Sunday Missal*, comp. Daughters of St. Paul (Boston: St. Paul Editions, 1974), p. 1088.

24. John 10:10.

25. Cited by John Ferraro, *Ten Series of Meditations on the Mysteries of the Rosary* (Boston: St. Paul Editions, 1964), p. 185.

26. John Paul II, Address to the Bishops of the United States, October 5, 1979, in *U.S.A.—The Message of Justice, Peace and Love*, pp. 188, 190.

27. Cited by John Ferraro, *Ten Series*, p. 171.

28. Ibid., p. 171.

29. Lamentations 5:21.

30. *Vatican II Sunday Missal*, pp. 604-605. Excerpt from the English translation of *The Roman*

Missal © 1973, International Committee on English in the Liturgy. All rights reserved.

31. Ibid., p. 622. Excerpt from the English translation of *The Roman Missal* © 1973, International Committee on English in the Liturgy. All rights reserved.

32. Ibid., pp. 622-623. Excerpt from the English translation of *The Roman Missal* © 1973, International Committee on English in the Liturgy. All rights reserved.

33. Titus 2:11-14.

34. *Sermo* 169, II, 13, cited by Ott, *Fundamentals of Catholic Dogma*, p. 252.

CONCLUSION

1. Titus 3:3-8.

2. John Paul II, Address to the Irish Youth, September 30, 1979, in *Ireland—"In the Footsteps of St. Patrick"* (Boston: St. Paul Editions, 1979), pp. 76-77.

3. Ibid., pp. 77-78.

BIBLIOGRAPHY

1. PRIMARY SOURCES

Maritain, Jacques. *Existence and the Existent*. Translated by Lewis Galantiere and Gerald B. Phelan. Garden City: Image Books, 1956.

_____. *Freedom in the Modern World*. Translated by Richard O'Sullivan, K.C. New York: Gordian Press, 1971.

_____. *God and the Permission of Evil*. Translated by Joseph W. Evans. Milwaukee: The Bruce Publishing Co., 1966.

_____. *On the Philosophy of History*. Translated by Joseph W. Evans. Clifton, New Jersey: Augustus M. Kelly, Publishers, 1973.

_____. *The Person and the Common Good*. Translated by John J. Fitzgerald. New York: Charles Scribner's Sons, 1947.

_____. *Ransoming the Time*. Translated by Harry Lorin Binsse. New York: Gordian Press, 1972.

_____. *St. Thomas and the Problem of Evil*. Milwaukee: Marquette University Press, 1942.

_____. *Three Reformers*. Port Washington, N.Y./London: Kennikat Press, 1970.

Thomas Aquinas, Saint. *Compendium of Theology*. Translated by Cyril Vollert, S.J. St. Louis: B. Herder Book Co., 1947: Chap. 115.

_____. *Summa Contra Gentiles:* "On the Truth of the Catholic Faith." Book I, translated by Anton C. Pegis; Book III, translated by Vernon J. Bourke. New York: Image Books, 1956. Bk. 1, chaps. 37, 41, 68, 71; bk. 3, chaps. 7-15, 111-117, 128.

_____. *Summa Theologiae*. Edited by Blackfriars. 60 vols. New York: McGraw-Hill Book Company, 1963. I, qq. 19; 23; 48, aa. 1, 2, 6; 49, a. 1, ad 3; 103, a. 7; I-II, qq. 75; 79; 90.

2. SECONDARY SOURCES

Alberione, Don Giacomo. *Carissimi in San Paolo*. Edited by Rosario F. Esposito, S.S.P. Roma: Edizioni Paoline, 1971.

Augustine, Saint. *Basic Writings of St. Augustine*. Edited by Whitney J. Oates. 2 vols. New York: Random House, 1948.

Confraternity of Christian Doctrine. *The Holy Bible*. Boston: St. Paul Editions, 1955.

Denzinger, Henricus and Adolfus Schönmetzer, S.I., eds. *Enchiridion Symbolorum*. Barcelona: Herder, 1963.

Ferraro, John. *Ten Series of Meditations on the Mysteries of the Rosary*. Boston: St. Paul Editions, 1964.

The Jerusalem Bible. Garden City, New York: Doubleday & Company, Inc. 1966.

John Paul II, Pope. *Catechesi Tradendae:* "Apostolic Exhortation on Catechesis in Our Time." Boston: St. Paul Editions, 1979.

_____. *Ireland—"In the Footsteps of St. Patrick."* Compiled and indexed by the Daughters of St. Paul. Boston: St. Paul Editions, 1979.

_____. *U.S.A.—The Message of Justice, Peace and Love.* Compiled and indexed by the Daughters of St. Paul. Boston: St. Paul Editions, 1979.

_____. *"You Are the Future, You Are My Hope."* Compiled and indexed by the Daughters of St. Paul. Boston: St. Paul Editions, 1979.

Journet, Charles. *The Meaning of Evil.* Translated by Michael Barry. New York: P.J. Kenedy & Sons, 1963.

Leo XIII, Pope. *Tametsi futura.* ASS, 33, 339, pp. 273-285.

L'Osservatore Romano. English edition. Vatican City, Europe.

Ott, Dr. Ludwig. *Fundamentals of Catholic Dogma.* Edited by James Canon Bastible. Rockford, Illinois: Tan Books and Publishers, Inc., 1974.

Sacred Congregation for the Clergy. *General Catechetical Directory.* Washington, D.C.: USCC Publications Office, 1971.

Vatican II. *The Sixteen Documents of Vatican II.* Boston: St. Paul Editions.

Vatican II Sunday Missal. Compiled by the Daughters of St. Paul. Boston: St. Paul Editions, 1974.

APPENDIX

The following text is from *God and the Permission of Evil*, by Jacques Maritain, p. 1, footnote 2:

> *Evil of nature*, or suffering, is the object neither of a *permission* nor of a *will properly so-called* of God—let us say rather that it is *admitted* by God, in this sense that from the very fact that God wills and causes, as transcendent first Cause, the good of the material universe and of the things of this universe, He causes at the same stroke, but *indirectly* and *per accidens* or in an *extra-intentional manner*, the losses and evils linked inevitably and by nature to the goods and to the gains in question (no generation without corruption, no life without some destruction, nor any passage to a superior form of life without some death—these are infrangible laws due to the very essence of material reality, and, analogically, of all created reality: *unless the grain of wheat...*).

Let us add that, created in the state of innocence, man found himself in the beginning preserved from death and suffering (although he had to "die the death of the angels" in sacrificing his own will in order to obey purposes which infinitely surpassed him). It is through his fault that he became subjugated to the laws of material nature, to suffering, and to death.

Daughters of St. Paul

IN MASSACHUSETTS
   50 St. Paul's Ave. Jamaica Plain, Boston, MA 02130;
      617-522-8911; 617-522-0875;
   172 Tremont Street, Boston, MA 02111; 617-426-5464;
      617-426-4230
IN NEW YORK
   78 Fort Place, Staten Island, NY 10301; 212-447-5071
   59 East 43rd Street, New York, NY 10017; 212-986-7580
   7 State Street, New York, NY 10004; 212-447-5071
   625 East 187th Street, Bronx, NY 10458; 212-584-0440
   525 Main Street, Buffalo, NY 14203; 716-847-6044
IN NEW JERSEY
   Hudson Mall — Route 440 and Communipaw Ave.,
      Jersey City, NJ 07304; 201-433-7740
IN CONNECTICUT
   202 Fairfield Ave., Bridgeport, CT 06604; 203-335-9913
IN OHIO
   2105 Ontario St. (at Prospect Ave.), Cleveland, OH 44115; 216-621-9427
   25 E. Eighth Street, Cincinnati, OH 45202; 513-721-4838
IN PENNSYLVANIA
   1719 Chestnut Street, Philadelphia, PA 19103; 215-568-2638
IN FLORIDA
   2700 Biscayne Blvd., Miami, FL 33137; 305-573-1618
IN LOUISIANA
   4403 Veterans Memorial Blvd., Metairie, LA 70002; 504-887-7631;
      504-887-0113
   1800 South Acadian Thruway, P.O. Box 2028, Baton Rouge, LA 70821
      504-343-4057; 504-343-3814
IN MISSOURI
   1001 Pine Street (at North 10th), St. Louis, MO 63101; 314-621-0346;
      314-231-5522
IN ILLINOIS
   172 North Michigan Ave., Chicago, IL 60601; 312-346-4228
IN TEXAS
   114 Main Plaza, San Antonio, TX 78205; 512-224-8101
IN CALIFORNIA
   1570 Fifth Avenue, San Diego, CA 92101; 714-232-1442
   46 Geary Street, San Francisco, CA 94108; 415-781-5180
IN HAWAII
   1143 Bishop Street, Honolulu, HI 96813; 808-521-2731
IN ALASKA
   750 West 5th Avenue, Anchorage AK 99501; 907-272-8183
IN CANADA
   3022 Dufferin Street, Toronto 395, Ontario, Canada
IN ENGLAND
   57, Kensington Church Street, London W. 8, England
IN AUSTRALIA
   58 Abbotsford Rd., Homebush, N.S.W., Sydney 2140, Australia